Grammar: A Friendly Approach

Grammar: A Friendly Approach

Christine Sinclair

Open University Press

06/09

Open University Press
McGraw-Hill Education
McGraw-Hill House
Shoppenhangers Road
Maidenhead
Berkshire
England
SL6 2QL

email: enquiries@openup.co.uk
world wide web: www.openup.co.uk

and Two Penn Plaza, New York, NY 10121-2289, USA

First published 2007

A catalogue record of this book is available from the British Library

ISBN-13: 978 0 335 22008 3 (pb)   978 0 335 22009 0 (hb)
ISBN-10: 0 335 22008 8 (pb)   0 335 22009 6 (hb)

Library of Congress Cataloguing-in-Publication Data
CIP data applied for

Typeset by RefineCatch Limited, Bungay, Suffolk
Printed in Poland by OZ Graf. S.A.
www.polskabook.pl

The McGraw·Hill Companies

For my father – Edward Patterson – who taught me about grammar . . . and not sneering.

With thanks to Jan Smith for reading and making helpful comments, and to Rowena Murray for her continuing support and encouragement.

Contents

List of figures

Part of speech	Description	Examples
Verb	Word showing action	be, do, have, learn, teach
Noun	Name of person, place, thing, idea	mother, Paris, table, existentialism
Pronoun	Word that stands for a noun	I, him, it, this, whose, someone, nobody
Adjective	Word that describes – usually goes with a noun or a pronoun	attractive, dusty, gentle, red
Articles	These are special types of adjective, showing whether the noun is indefinite or definite.	
	Indefinite	a, an
	Definite	the
Adverb	Word that modifies a verb or adjective, or other adverb (often ends in -ly)	fully, gracefully, usually, very
Preposition	Word that indicates a relationship	for, through, to, up
Conjunction	Joining word	and, but, or (joining expressions of equal importance – coordinating) because, though, when (joining something less to something more important – subordinating)
Interjection	Word expressing emotion which is unrelated to the rest of the sentence (usually not appropriate for academic writing)	alas, ha-ha, wowee

FIGURE (i) Parts of speech. Appendix 1 provides more details on verbs, nouns, pronouns, adjectives and adverbs.

This page shows some of the issues from the book in a simplified visual form, especially those from Chapters 6 to 8. There may also be other things, such as complements and phrases. See the Glossary for the meanings of all of these words.

1. Simple sentence

You might also see this called a principal clause, a main clause, or an independent clause. There is often an object, but not always.

2. Compound sentence

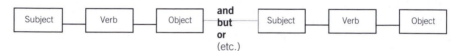

3. Complex sentence

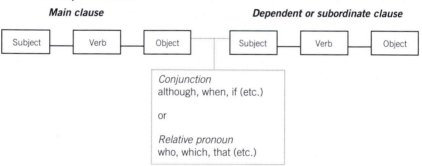

FIGURE (ii) Building blocks of sentences. There are more details in Appendix 2 on types of clause: adverbial, relative and noun clauses.

1

Introduction

1.1 Why the book was written • 1.2 How the book is structured • 1.3 How to annoy your lecturers • 1.4 Meet the students • 1.5 Conclusion: comments about grammar and language

- *What is this book trying to do?*
- *What are the usual errors with grammar and language?*

This is a good time for grammar and punctuation. Lynne Truss's runaway success with *Eats, Shoots & Leaves* shows that people welcome high standards in language use and want to ensure that we can all communicate clearly and effectively. After years when many schools did not teach grammar explicitly, the subject has started to reappear. A number of writers are now showing us that it does not have to be a dry, dull subject.

This book is for all university or college students who have been told that they 'need to do something about grammar' or are worried that their grammar is not up to scratch. It is also for anyone who is interested in grammar and how it works, including school students. Some school teachers and college or university lecturers feel anxious about grammar too: you might be surprised at how many.

The term 'grammar' has a broad meaning here, including language use and punctuation as well as sentence structure. The book is not as comprehensive as some other grammar books, and there are suggestions for further reading in the Bibliography. Its purpose is different from those books.

1.1 Why the book was written

I have worked in three different universities – ancient, modern, and a former polytechnic. In all three, I have seen many students who have problems with grammar and use of language. Although there are some excellent books on grammar and punctuation, the students who come to see me often tell me that they don't know where to start with them. There are too many technical terms to learn and rules that seem to be broken all the time.

Grammar and punctuation do not just exist as sets of arbitrary rules to annoy students who are writing essays; they help us to make sense of the world. Most of us are able to use excellent grammatical structures without too much thought, especially when we're speaking. There are just a few typical muddles when people write things down and this book attempts to cover the most common difficulties.

I wanted to write the book because I thought that students need advice set in the kind of context that actually happens. I have tried to bring the issues alive by making them happen to three students: Abel, Barbara and Kim. These characters are based on real students that I meet – especially their problems and their responses to them. To give the context a bit of a story, I have added some details about the students' lives that I would not normally hear about. This is a grammar book with a soap opera in it.

1.2 How the book is structured

Each chapter is devoted to a particular issue related to language, grammar or punctuation. It starts with a story, where one or more of the students faces the issue and tries to resolve it. There are then some questions to encourage you to think where you are with this topic and some advice, which might involve more bits of the story. The stories build up over the book, but you can also read them as individual scenes.

The language used in the book itself is informal – I am not writing in an academic style. However, there are also some technical terms. A lot of grammar is about naming types of words and the relationships between them. It can be useful for you to know about the technical terms, in case anyone uses them with you, for example in giving feedback on an essay. At the end of each chapter, I have suggested the terms that you could look up in more comprehensive grammar books or on the World Wide Web, where there are many useful sites.

There is a Glossary at the end of the book where you can look up specific topics, and it tells you which chapters you can find them in. So, for example, if you have been having problems with *commas*, the Glossary will direct you to Chapter 9 and particularly draw your attention to Figure 9.1, which looks at the functions of different punctuation marks. If it appears in the Glossary, a word is in italics the first time it is used. As well as the Glossary, two appendices contain expansions of some grammatical terms for those who are interested.

The book can be read in several ways, depending on your needs. You can read it right through and see the stories and the grammatical points build up. The more complex grammatical points tend to be later in the book. Alternatively, if you want to get information about a particular point, you might use the Contents list, the Glossary or the Index to find out where that point is likely to be.

At the start of each chapter I have indicated the main questions that relate to the chapter. These can be seen together in Figure 1.1. You'll notice that some are in bold type: these are questions that I think you could most usefully ask yourself when you are trying to write something. The emphasis, though, is on getting things written first and then checking it for a reader later – one of the problems with teaching grammar is that it makes students freeze and not write anything! I certainly don't want to have that effect.

Each chapter concludes with a summary of the main advice given in the chapter. If you are in a real hurry, you might just want to go straight to the conclusion of the chapter.

1.3 How to annoy your lecturers

I asked a group of lecturers from different subject areas what really annoyed them about students' grammar and language use. Figure 1.2 shows their top ten pet hates.

Each of these topics is considered in this book. Here's a quick reference to where to find the information.

1 The apostrophe has a chapter of its own – Chapter 10
2 Chapter 2 looks at easily confused words, especially in section 2.4
3 Chapter 2 also has some general advice about spelling
4 You'll find some comments on informal language in Chapter 2 too.
5 Chapters 4 and 5 look at verbs; Chapter 7 deals with sentences
6 Section 7.7 looks at the relationship between sentences and paragraphs
7 If you don't know what a paragraph is, you'll find out in Chapter 7
8 Chapters 7 and 8 should help you avoid convoluted sentences
9 Chapter 2 has warnings about pompous language
10 Section 7.6 deals with *comma splices*; Chapter 9 also considers commas

Chapter	Questions
1	What is this book trying to do?
	What are the usual errors with grammar and language?
2	What goes wrong with words?
	What exactly are you trying to say?
3	Why do you need to know about *Standard English*?
	How does your use of *participles* say something about you?
4	**What's going on?** Or is it over?
	Should you write in the past, present or future?
5	What's the difference between *active* and *passive*?
	How can you write in an impersonal way?
6	Who or what is doing things?
	Who or what is having things done to them?
7	What is a sentence?
	Is there a *subject, verb, object*?
	What gives you a clue that your sentences might be wrong?
	How do sentences work together?
8	Are you commenting on the action, subject or anything else?
	Are you defining or describing something else in the sentence?
	Which words are your signposts?
9	Does your punctuation show the reader how groups of words should be read?
	Does your punctuation complete, introduce, separate, enclose, or omit?
10	Do you need punctuation to join, abbreviate or omit letters in words?
	What use is the *apostrophe*?
11	Do you understand what the grammar checker is telling you?

FIGURE 1.1 Questions associated with each chapter. The ones in bold are particularly useful to have in mind when you are writing.

1.4 Meet the students

The experiences of three students highlight the grammatical issues in the book. These students went to an informal essay-writing session held at their university soon after Christmas and discovered that they had something in common: they were all getting pulled up for their grammar but didn't

Lecturers really hate it when you…

1 Use apostrophes wrongly
2 Confuse common words, for example, there/their
3 Make spelling errors
4 Use informal language
5 Write sentences without verbs
6 Make every sentence a paragraph
7 Don't use paragraphs
8 Write long convoluted sentences
9 Try to write too pompously
10 Use *run-on sentences*/comma splices

FIGURE 1.2 What annoys lecturers most.

know what they could do about it. Here is some background information about them.

Barbara is 18 and in her first year, studying philosophy, English and sociology. She is enjoying university life and being away from home for the first time. In the first semester, she spent more time thinking about her emotional life than her essay writing. She split up with a boyfriend at home just before she arrived and met a guy called Mark during Freshers Week, went out with him a few times but hasn't heard from him for six weeks. She is trying not to let this put her off her studies and has started the second semester determined to improve her grades.

Abel is a second year student, studying science – mainly physics and biology. He had a few years out before he came to university; he is 25. This semester he is taking an elective on the philosophy of science, which he is finding strangely intriguing, and he is starting to question his choice of subjects and what he wants to do with his degree. He is wondering about becoming a teacher, an idea that would have been totally alien to him a few years ago. He feels that if he doesn't improve his language skills, he is going to limit the options open to him.

Kim is in her final year, hoping to graduate with a good degree in mechanical engineering. In her first couple of years she was irritated by comments about her writing – 'I'm not at University to do English!' However, she now recognizes that engineers have to be able to express themselves clearly too, and as she is thinking about doing further study (possibly a PhD), she needs to do something about her difficulties with writing. She has particular problems with punctuation, but she doesn't understand why people make such a fuss about it. She is just coming up for 21 and planning a big party to celebrate.

We'll also meet some of their other friends and relatives and find out a bit more about their personalities during each chapter. Here's an extract from the conversation they have after the essay-writing class. It's pouring with rain when they come out and they run to the café for shelter and coffee.

Abel:	I keep getting told that my *syntax* is poor. That would be OK if I knew what it meant!
Kim:	I get that one as well. I thought a syntax error was something to do with computing but apparently it can just mean your grammar's not good.
Barbara:	I looked it up, 'cause I got it as well. It does mean something to do with grammar and sentences – the structure of a sentence. And in computing it's the rules for combining bits of a programming language. So it's similar.
Abel:	Where did you look it up – have you got quite a good dictionary?
Barbara:	Yes – my parents gave me one at Christmas and I was like, great – what do I want that for? But now I'm glad they did; I'm using it loads. I got a *thesaurus* too.
Abel:	What does that do?
Barbara:	Well, you look it up if you want to find words that are grouped together, or *synonyms*, you know – have the same meaning.
Kim:	I've got a scientific dictionary – it's quite good. But it doesn't help me with punctuation. Someone gave me a book about that, but I don't understand it.
Abel:	I've just bought a grammar book, but I don't really like it. I started to read it and fell asleep.
Barbara:	It's good to find other people with the same problems. I've been a bit embarrassed to talk about it. Some of the lecturers seem to put you down if your grammar's not right – you know, they're a bit sneering. I was wondering if there'd be any grammar classes, but you don't like to ask.
Abel:	Well, I've just learned a whole load talking to you two – about dictionaries, syntax, synonyms . . . any other 'syns' you want to tell me about? Listen, do you fancy meeting here again another day – I'll bring my grammar book – and we can talk about essays and stuff.

Barbara's very keen on this idea. Kim isn't so sure (Abel's comments on 'syns' has put her off) but they do all arrange to meet a couple of days later and read each others' assignments that have to be handed in over the next week. They all agree that the basic rule is 'no sneering'.

1.5 Conclusion: comments about grammar and language

- It's not your fault if you were not taught grammar at school. It is important to try to get it right now, though.
- The same grammatical errors keep coming up in students' essays. It is useful to know what these are so that you can take steps to avoid them.
- It's a good idea to have a dictionary that is appropriate for the subjects you are studying. A thesaurus can be useful too, but should be used with care (as you'll see in Chapter 2).
- You can learn a lot from talking to other students. You can also give each other reassurance.

1.5.1 Technical terms relating to this chapter

For further information, look up these words in the Glossary, other grammar books or the World Wide Web.

Synonym
Syntax
Thesaurus

2

Bad language

- *What goes wrong with words?*
- *What exactly are you trying to say?*

Kuhn further condemns Popper's claim that when a paradigm is falsified it is dishevelled. The occurrence of an old paradigm tergiversation depends on the availability of a novel one. In other words, Popper retorts that when the the raft is uninhabitable we jump into the sea, while Kuhn stresses the

?

When you become a university student, you have to learn how to speak and write like the experts in your subject do. It can take students a while to realize this; some feel, for instance, that it is phoney to try to write as a sociologist or a chemical engineer when you're just starting. Some students will try to imitate the style and the attempt doesn't quite work. There seems to be a tension between the writing that you are used to and the writing that you have to do when you're an expert in the subject. It is natural and normal to experience this tension and to have to find your way through it.

Our story illustrates some of the dangers of trying to put fancy words into an essay. Abel has just bought himself a thesaurus and thinks that it is going to solve some of his problems.

2.1 Abel tries to be posh

Abel is waiting impatiently in the café for the others. He's been fired up with the writing he has been doing on paradigm shifts in science and can't wait to show the others what he has done. When Barbara arrives he gives her his draft and watches her reaction. She doesn't seem as excited as he is by the subject and in fact looks puzzled.

Barbara: I don't think this is going to work. I don't understand a word of this. Maybe it's because it's about science.

Abel: But it's the philosophy of science. You're doing philosophy too.

Barbara: Well, what does this mean? 'Kuhn further condemns Popper's claim that when a paradigm is falsified it is dishevelled.' What's a 'dishevelled paradigm' when it's at home?

Abel: Let's see? Oh that's something I got from a book but I changed some of the words. I was looking for another word for 'abandoned' and that sounded quite a good one. Found it in a thesaurus. Maybe it's not quite right though.

Barbara: It's not right – have you got the book there?

Abel hands Barbara *The Ascent of Science* by Brian Silver. He's marked page 105 where he's used large chunks of two paragraphs about Kuhn and Popper.

Barbara: Abel – you've just copied this and changed the odd word. And it doesn't make sense. And this other bit's your own and you're just putting in fancy words for the sake of it.

Kim arrives with an engineering report under her arm.

> | | |
> |---|---|
> | *Kim:* | Oh, you're hard at it already. Just got myself a thesaurus – they're great. |
> | *Barbara:* | Well, don't do what Abel's just done – he's used it to turn a good piece of writing into crap. |
> | *Abel:* | Wait a minute – no sneering, remember. |
> | *Barbara:* | Well, OK, but you really can't just use a thesaurus like that. |

See what you think yourself of Abel's attempt to use a thesaurus (Figure 2.1). As you read his version of Brian Silver's original, think about how a lecturer might read it.

2.2 Questions about language

1 What errors in language use would you pick out in Abel's writing?
2 How does Brian Silver's piece use the idea of rafts? Should Abel be using it the same way?

The following sections consider typical language errors, including some of the ones in Abel's writing. There are suggested answers to those two questions in Section 2.9. There are also alternative versions of what Abel is trying to say there.

2.3 Idioms – how words are usually used

Some of the examples I am using are ones I have actually seen. A student I saw replaced the word 'abandoned' with 'dishevelled' and I had to explain to her that the only time such a substitution would be appropriate would be when talking about someone's hair or clothes. It was not idiomatic for her to write about a system of government being dishevelled.

By 'idiomatic', I mean 'the way we usually say it'. Idiom means the distinctive use of language that does not relate particularly to the dictionary meaning of the words used (for example, think about the expression 'kick the bucket'). As with the example of 'abandoned', idiomatic use usually relates to which words can be appropriately used together. Use of correct idiom is often a problem for international students, because English has some very strange expressions. Idiom can also be different in different areas of the UK and it changes over

Original writing

Kuhn further rejects Popper's claim that when a paradigm is falsified it is abandoned. According to Kuhn, abandonment of an old paradigm occurs only when a new one is available. In other words, Popper says that when the raft is uninhabitable we jump into the sea, while Kuhn says we jump only when another raft is available.

Popper, in reply, concedes that much science is not carried out with the object of falsifying theories, and he sees such science as second-class. He insists that science as a whole jumps forward by the process of falsification.

(Silver 1998: 105)

Abel's version and additional comment

Kuhn further condemns Popper's claim that when a paradigm is falsified it is dishevelled. The occurrence of an old paradigm tergiversation depends on the availability of a novel one. In other words, Popper retorts that when the the raft is uninhabitable we jump into the sea, while Kuhn stresses the availability of a further raft.

Popper, in reply, is lenient about science that does not have falsification but regards it as second class. He is obstinate that science as a hole jumps forward by the process of falsification.

This postulation of differences illustrate the intransigencies of the two writers and the difficulties of the determination of the shifting of a paradigm. It is the author's opinion that falsification is not a necessity but it is something that should be essayed by scientists in there deliberations.

FIGURE 2.1 Dangerous use of a thesaurus (and other language errors).

time. Academic subjects have their own idioms and it can take some time to get used to them.

If you are unfamiliar with the idiomatic use of a word, then you may cause confusion when you use it as a replacement.

2.4 Easily confused words

One of the most common errors students make is to confuse 'their', 'there' and 'they're'. You may have noticed that Abel had used the wrong one in his last sentence. It is easily done, especially if you are the sort of writer who hears words in your head before you write them down. Like Abel, I also often confuse these words if I am writing quickly, but have trained myself to make a mental check that I am using the correct one. It helps to think that the word 'here' is often present in easily confused words that refer to place:

Here	in this place	Hear	use the ear
There	in that place	They're	short for they are
Where	in which place	Were	past tense of are

There are many easily confused words. It is not always so easy to find ways of distinguishing them. In Figure 2.2, I have made some suggestions where I can.

These are errors I have particularly noticed. You can find longer lists of these words in some other books, for example Burt (2004). (See the Bibliography at the end of the book for details.)

Notice that Abel also used 'hole' instead of 'whole' even when he was copying from someone else's writing. If he had checked this carefully, he would probably have recognized that it was wrong; to a lecturer, however, the misspelling just looks illiterate rather than poor checking.

2.5 Singulars and plurals

'This postulation of differences illustrate the intransigencies of the two writers . . .'

Apart from being rather pompous, this extract from Abel's essay demonstrates a very common language error – a plural verb is used when a singular was needed. It is the postulation that illustrates the intransigencies. Alternatively (and more readably) Abel could have written:

These differences illustrate . . .

This point relates to how a sentence is put together – using a subject and a verb. There is more on this in Chapter 6.

Singular subject	*This postulation* of differences illustrates . . .
Plural subject	*These differences* illustrate . . .

This word...	which means...	is often confused with...	which means...
affect	(to) act upon or influence (verb)	effect	the result of an action (noun)
	Less commonly, it means emotion (noun)		Less commonly, it means to bring about a result (verb)
compliment	praise	complement	complete/completion
its	belonging to it	it's	it is
			Tip: never use 'it's' in academic writing
practise	(to) work at or carry out (verb)	practice	action or performance (noun)
			There are other examples where the s is in the verb and the c in the noun – in the first one, we can hear the difference:
			advise/advice license/licence
principle	an origin or rule (noun)	principal	main (adjective)
			head of a university or college (noun)
your	belonging to you	you're	you are
			Tip: don't use *abbreviations* or 'you' in academic writing

FIGURE 2.2 Some easily confused words.

2.6 Formal or pompous?

When you are at university, you are expected to write formally. Some broad rules for this are:

- **Don't use abbreviations such as 'don't'!**
  You'll notice that I'm not attempting to write formally in this book.
- **Avoid slang words and clichés.**
  Clichés are hackneyed or overused expressions such as 'in this day and age', 'the writing on the wall'.
- **Avoid words or expressions with emotional or extreme overtones.**
  If you feel that you should use an exclamation mark, then the expression is probably inappropriate.

There is a big difference, though, between avoiding slang and using pompous expressions. In his excitement with the riches of the thesaurus, Abel came across the word 'tergiversate' which means 'to turn one's back; to desert, change sides; to shuffle, shift, use evasions' (*Chambers Dictionary*, 2003). While this might seem appropriate for writing about paradigm shifts, there is a good chance that it would not be idiomatic use. Abel has never seen the word in context so he does not know. The lecturer would probably have to look the word up. The main effect is likely to be a comic one or an irritation, depending on the personality and mood of the lecturer. Abel is unlikely to impress the lecturer with this word.

One of the problems in writing about language is that we like to tell you what you can't do, but that doesn't help you to decide what words you are able to use. So Abel is understandably upset at Barbara's apparent sneering – breaking the group's main rule – which doesn't help him at all to work out what he could be saying. A simple question from Kim saves the day:

'What exactly is it that you're trying to say?'

Here is Abel's reply:

Well, a paradigm shift is when the whole way of thinking about something changes – like when people realized that the earth goes round the sun instead of the sun going round the earth. That meant that everything had to be rethought. But it wasn't a sudden thing – Copernicus suggested it, then Galileo took it up later and had real problems with the Church because of it. Popper says that when a scientific explanation has been shown to be false, that's when we abandon it. He thinks it's important that we keep trying to falsify scientific thinking, because that's how we advance. But Kuhn's argument is that we need another framework to replace it – you don't get rid of one explanation until you have another one.

I think they're both right: you should try to look for counter examples or other ways of falsifying the way we think. But you might not find them. As well as trying to show that something's false, it's also useful to look for other ways of saying things. So I don't think it's necessary to prove things false – you don't have to do it – but it's useful to try. The main point of my essay is that we have to be careful that we don't become trapped by our existing ways of looking at things. If everyone just proves what they know already, then science never moves on.

Like many students, Abel finds that he can say it but he can't write it. As soon as he starts to write his own opinion, he gets caught up in whether or not he's entitled to do so. Should he call himself 'the author', for instance?

2.7 The author, one or I?

In much academic writing, the use of 'I' (the first *person* singular) is not acceptable. People use a lot of different ways to get round this. Repeated use of 'the author' can be very tedious, though it can be useful at the start of a piece of writing; for example:

This report was written to record the findings from the author's placement at x during the summer of [date].

Often, it is possible to avoid saying 'I' at all. Students frequently want to write 'I believe that ...' or 'it is my opinion that ...' If you find you have written an expression like this in your first draft, then score out these words. You will be left with a statement. Then you should consider whether you have any evidence or good reasons for making such a statement.

Examples:

(a) poverty is a major cause of ill-health.
(b) falsification is not necessary.

In example (a), the student might look for statistics or other evidence from books to back up this claim. It may be necessary to tone it down a little by saying something such as: 'Statistics suggest that there is a strong association between poverty and ill-health.' You would also have to include a reference to your source of information for these statistics.

In example (b), Abel has his own reason for suggesting that falsification is not necessary but should still be attempted. He might end up with a statement such as: 'Falsification may not be necessary for scientific progress because alternative explanations can still arise without it.' In this case, he is giving a reason rather than evidence, though it still might be useful to add some examples if he can.

2.8 Do engineers use the same language as social scientists?

Abel suddenly realizes that he understands more about Kuhn and Popper than he has thought and that the answer is not just to cobble together bits from the books.

Abel: Kim – you're great. I'm going to ask myself that whenever I'm stuck. 'What exactly is it that you're trying to say?' Do you do that yourself?

Kim: Yeah – I've always found that useful. Then I have to take out all the stuff like 'I' and 'me' and make it sound neutral. Engineers hate you to use 'I'.

Abel: So do scientists. Perhaps you can do it in some subjects?

Barbara: The study skills lecturer said that it's usually best to avoid it. But there was a social work student at the class who said she sometimes has to say 'I' 'cause they do a lot of reflective writing.

Kim: Reflective, eh? Don't fancy that. I don't really have problems with the words themselves. It's more punctuation for me. Can't spell them, of course. I'm always getting 'gauge' wrong and apparently it really annoys the lecturers.

Barbara: My sister's doing business studies and she can't spell 'business'! My problem's psychology – I never know where to put the h. That's why I chose sociology!

Kim: I suppose we should really get to grips with the words of our own subjects – the ones we're going to keep using. Both how to spell them and how they're used in context. But I don't think you need to bother remembering 'tergiversation' Abel. Don't think you'll need to use that one a lot.

Abel: I'm really glad I chose this module, though. It's giving me a different way of seeing the world. The way some of the stuff is written is very different from the strictly science books. I quite like it, but there are a lot more words rather than equations and stuff.

Kim: I couldn't be bothered with that – I like illustrations and equations.

> Give me science and engineering any time. That's why I don't like writing – I'd rather do some calculations or draw something.
>
> *Barbara:* But don't engineers still have to write big reports?
>
> *Kim:* Yeah – I've got a short one here but it's my final year project I'm most worried about. Right – you're getting an invite to my party, both of you – but only if you help me with the commas for the report I've just wrote.
>
> *Barbara:* You've just wrote? Don't you mean you have just written?
>
> *Abel:* No sneering, Barbara. Remember?
>
> *Barbara:* Not sneering – just pointing out.
>
> *Kim:* Whatever.

2.9 Comments on questions

1 What errors in language use would you pick out in Abel's writing?

- The main error he has made is that he has plagiarized someone else's writing. Changing the odd word is not enough.
- In particular, his word substitution is inappropriate. The following words are not idiomatic for their context: condemns, dishevelled, tergiversation, retorts, obstinate, lenient.
- He has accidentally repeated a word (the).
- He has misspelled two words that sound like others: hole for whole and there for their.
- When he uses 'the author's opinion', it is a little confusing. He could be referring to Popper, though a little thought shows he is referring to himself. But it trips the reader up to have to work this out.

2 How does Brian Silver's piece use the idea of rafts? Should Abel be using it the same way?

The rafts have been used as a *metaphor* (see Glossary) to illustrate Silver's point. If Abel uses the same metaphor without acknowledgement, it is likely to draw attention to his *plagiarism*. Metaphors can stand out, especially if they do not fit a student's own style of writing. This metaphor is a particularly useful one, however, as it highlights the idea of a 'container' or 'framework' to support our perspective on the world. The second example below shows how to acknowledge someone else's metaphor.

Alternative ways of writing the section of Abel's essay

1 The work of two writers, Popper and Kuhn, illustrates different ways of explaining scientific advances. While Popper argues that scientists abandon a principle when it has been shown to be false, Kuhn believes that they do not abandon it until there is another to replace it. Kuhn's work on paradigm shifts suggests that scientists are bound by the paradigms of their own time and place. Although these views are apparently opposing, they both offer some insights into scientific history. Falsification may not be necessary for scientific progress because alternative explanations of the world have arisen without it. It may still be useful, though, to consider both Popper's encouragement to demonstrate that our principles are not false and Kuhn's concerns about the difficulties of seeing beyond our current paradigm.

2 Silver (1998) uses the metaphor of a raft to illustrate the difference between the views of Popper and Kuhn. The raft is the scientific framework, or paradigm. For Popper, the raft becomes uninhabitable – or the scientific framework has been falsified – and scientists have to jump into the sea. For Kuhn, scientists will not abandon the raft unless there is another one. This metaphor usefully highlights two questions: do scientists have to have a paradigm, and do they have to falsify it before they get a new one? Falsification may not be necessary for scientific progress because alternative explanations of the world have arisen without it. Nevertheless, it may be useful for scientists to attempt to falsify paradigms to avoid being stuck with their current ways of thinking.

2.10 Conclusion: advice about word choice

- Become familiar with words that are easily confused and train yourself to spot them.
- Avoid the extremes of slang and pompous writing.
- Think about what you are trying to say, rather than trying to drag an essay from books.
- Don't use an alternative word from a thesaurus or dictionary unless you are familiar with its idiomatic use.
- Learn how to spell the frequently used words in your own subject area.
- You'll get into the way of writing in your subject's style as you grow more familiar with its idioms. If you read a lot, it will help your writing.

2.10.1 Technical terms relating to this chapter

For further information, look up these words in the Glossary, other grammar books or the World Wide Web.

Idiom
Metaphor
Plagiarism

3

Mangling and dangling participles

3.1 Why can't I use my own language? • 3.2 Questions about 'correct' English • 3.3 Standard English – do we need it? • 3.4 Participles – present and past • 3.5 No dangling! • 3.6 Kim has seen the light, has written and has gone • 3.7 Comments on questions • 3.8 Conclusion: advice about participles

- *Why do you need to know about **Standard English**?*
- *How does your use of participles say something about you?*

Participles are bits of verbs. They cause some problems because they are used differently in different *dialects*.

3.1 Why can't I use my own language?

Kim: What's wrong with 'I've wrote' anyway? Everyone says that.

The students are finding it difficult to give each other constructive advice. They don't know each other well enough yet to feel totally relaxed about teasing, and criticism of what people say can sometimes be taken for 'sneering' even when it's not meant that way. The argument later shows the problems.

Barbara:	It's just wrong. It's ignorant and illiterate. My mum and dad went over it and over it when I was a kid. If ever I said, 'I've went' or 'I been' they corrected me every time. So I just know it's wrong.
Abel:	So when is it right to say 'wrote'? Is it when you say 'have' before it? So it should be: I have written, I have gone, I have done . . . Or I wrote, I went, I did.
Kim:	Barbara, I listen to the football on BBC radio nearly every Saturday. Just last week, they were talking about my team – the team has went from strength to strength. I remember it clearly.
Barbara:	They're just plain wrong. Illiterate. That's footballers for you.
Abel:	And what happens with 'of' instead of 'have'?
Barbara:	What do you mean 'of'?
Abel:	Is it 'I should of went' or 'I should of gone'?
Barbara:	It shouldn't be 'of' at all Abel. That's just pure nonsense. It's 'have'. I should have gone. Why would you say 'of'? It doesn't make sense.
Kim:	I think it must have changed, Barbara. If it's on the radio, it must be OK.
Barbara:	No it's not. I have a lot of problems with grammar but I do know this one. It was footballers my dad used to complain about when they came on TV. He said they were illiterate and got paid too much money. He kept saying that I had to get this right or I'd not get into uni.
Kim:	Well, that's a load of rubbish then, 'cause I'm here and I get it wrong. Sounds like snobbery and sneering to me.
Abel:	Me too. I think it might be old-fashioned. And round here, most people say a mix of I've went or I've gone. Everyone understands you so why does it matter?
Barbara:	Course it matters. You've got to have standards. And the educated way is 'I have gone'. I'm going to keep saying it and saying it until you've got it into your thick heads.
Kim:	Oh shut up Barbara; you're being a snob. And go and get us another coffee.
Barbara:	[*Storms off and shouts over her shoulder*] I have gone; I have gone; I have gone.

3.2 Questions about 'correct' English

1 Should we accept local usages of words in colleges and universities rather than insisting on 'correct' English?

2 Do you know the 'correct' forms of past versions of bring, do, go, see, write? What about the past of the verb 'to be'?
3 Why am I writing 'correct' in quotation marks?

There are comments on these questions in Section 3.7. There is also more detail about saying things in the past in the next chapter.

3.3 Standard English – do we need it?

Standard English refers to 'the form of English taught in schools, etc., and used, esp. in formal situations, by the majority of educated English-speakers' (*Chambers Dictionary*, 2003).

Many of the writers who comment on Standard English point out that it is just one dialect of English. (For a definition of 'dialect', see the Glossary and for examples of writers who talk about language and power, see the Bibliography.) Standard English is the dominant dialect and the one used by the most powerful people in the UK. If you want to be acknowledged as a 'correct' speaker by educated English speakers, you need to be able to use the correct *past participles* of verbs – the bits that are causing Kim so much difficulty.

If Standard English is just the dialect that is most successful, and is associated with power, then there is a political aspect to its use. Some people might make a case for saying that another dialect would be more appropriate. As Kim pointed out, other dialects are also heard on radio and television. For example, at the end of the 1990s and start of the present century, the steeplejack Fred Dibnah presented a number of programmes on UK television about the history of engineering and used a local dialect in his presentations that would not be regarded as Standard English. In particular, he could frequently be heard saying 'it were' instead of the standard version 'it was'. Yet his programmes were regarded as educational. So does this mean that we no longer need to bother?

Like Barbara, I grew up with parents who immediately corrected any use of English that was not standard, except when I was using it for particular effect – perhaps a joke. They also commented on 'bad' English used by popular entertainers. This does mean that I hardly ever make these mistakes myself, so I am protected from the judgement that I am 'uneducated' because of the way I speak.

I don't always take such a strong line myself, however. My main concern is that people are able to make themselves understood and I recognize that the language is constantly changing. Even so, if people do make judgements about students because of their past participles – and I know that they do because they have told me so – then I firmly believe that those students have a right to know about it. They have a right to decide whether or not they want to use the dominant dialect that gives the impression that they are educated speakers.

The next section, then, contains some of what you need to know about participles.

3.4 Participles – present and past

work – verb
working – present participle
worked – past participle

Participles are parts of verbs. They are used in various forms relating to the past, present and future and we shall look at those particularly in Chapter 4. Here, we are more concerned with using the correct form and spelling.

Present participles are easy, in one way (though they do have their own problems, which we start to look at in Section 3.5 later and then consider later in Chapter 7). Present participles always end in -ing. Sometimes people get confused because they involve doubling a letter, or removing an e, to get the right sound. A very small number just don't quite follow the rules. See the examples in Figure 3.1.

Past participles are often formed by adding -ed. If there is already an e, then it's just a d that is added. Again, there can be doubling of letters – and many counter examples. In the examples in Figure 3.2, notice that you can say 'I have . . .' before each.

Students' spelling problems are often associated with gaining or losing letters from participles such as the ones in Figures 3.1 and 3.2. In the next

Just add -ing	Double a letter	Lose an e	Odd
being	cutting	advising	dying
bringing	getting	coming	dyeing
doing	hopping	filing	panicking
falling	nodding	hoping	
filling	sinning	judging	
going	stirring	noticing	
playing	stopping	practising	
seeing		shining	
singing		writing	
singeing			
studying			
working			

FIGURE 3.1 Present participles.

Add -ed	Add just d	Double a letter	Odd/irregular
filled	advised	hopped	been
played	died	nodded	brought
worked	dyed	sinned	come
	filed	stirred	done
You may need	hoped	stopped	gone
to change a y to	judged		got
an i before	noticed		fallen
adding the -ed	practised		led
	singed		panicked
emptied			read
studied			seen
			shone
			sung
			written

FIGURE 3.2 Past participles.

two sections, we look at some other participle problems – Barbara's with the present and Kim's with the past.

3.5 No dangling!

Barbara wasn't too happy to get a comment on an essay that said '*dangling participle!*', especially after she'd made such a fuss about getting past participles right. It's usually the present participle that gets dangled, when it's being used to modify another part of the sentence. Here's Barbara's example:

Being a man of considerable means, Jane Austen wanted Mr Darcey to be the focus of attention.

When she talked to Kim about it, Kim thought she could see what the lecturer meant. 'It looks as if you're saying that Jane Austen was a man of considerable means.'

Barbara didn't think it did, but when she looked up 'dangling participle' in some books, she realized that if you have a word such as 'being', it should relate to the main part of the sentence appropriately. It did look as though she was saying that Jane Austen was a man!

Here are some alternatives.

Being a man of considerable means, Mr Darcey was used by Jane Austen as a focus of attention.

Jane Austen wanted Mr Darcey, being a man of considerable means, to be the focus of attention.

The problem with starting a sentence with a present participle is that the reader immediately wonders who or what this expression relates to. If it is *misrelated* (or dangling) then it trips the reader up. It can lead to unconscious humour, for example:

Reading about Africa, the lion seems to be the main predator.

(Which books are the lions reading?)

Sipping a cold beer, my golden retriever was at my feet and my book was open at my favourite poem.

(Did the dog and book share the beer?)

3.6 Kim has seen the light, has written and has gone

Kim has arranged to meet the others in the café after she sees her tutor about her plans for her dissertation. When she hasn't turned up, Barbara starts to worry.

Barbara: I wonder where she's got to. She wasn't very happy earlier; I hope that man's not upset her.

Abel: What man? Is she seeing someone?

Barbara: No, just her tutor. She doesn't like him. She overheard him talking about someone. He was, like, 'We can't let her do the presentation to the industrial sponsors because her grammar's so awful'.

Abel: Was he talking about Kim?

Barbara: I hope not. Imagine hearing that about yourself. Oh, wait . . . she's just texted me. What's she saying? '*I saw my tutor. He was talking about me, but I am doing the presentation. I'm writing this in the library. I've come to find a book about participles. CU later. Kim.*' Well, she's used the right participles in this text. In fact, this is the most understandable text she's ever sent!

Abel: She shouldn't be using her phone in the library though. She'll get done for bleeping, especially when you send a reply.

Barbara: Well, at least you didn't say, 'she'll get did for bleeping!'

3.7 Comments on questions

1 Should we accept local usages of words in colleges and universities rather than insisting on 'correct' English?

This is quite a sensitive issue and you'll probably already be aware that I am sympathetic to people who have not been brought up with Standard English as their main dialect.

It is probably appropriate, however, for institutions to encourage certain standards of writing for several reasons:

- students do not just come from the local area but from other parts of the country and from other countries too;
- consistency in language use helps to ensure accuracy and shared meaning;
- the outside world expects certain standards of language use in graduates;
- you may create a poor impression of yourself if you don't use the Standard English terms.

The key issue in all these reasons is that we use language to communicate.

2 Do you know the 'correct' forms of past versions of bring, do, go, see, write? What about the past of the verb 'to be'?

There are several ways you might have answered this, depending on whether you used the simple past or one with an *auxiliary verb* such as 'have' or 'has'. There is more on auxiliary verbs in the next chapter.

	Past tense	Perfect tense (see Glossary)
Bring	I brought	I have brought
Do	I did	I have done
Go	I went	I have gone
See	I saw	I have seen
Write	I wrote	I have written
Be	I was	I have been

FIGURE 3.3 Past and perfect tense of some irregular verbs.

3 Why am I writing 'correct' in quotation marks?

The use of scare quotes draws attention to my view that being correct is not a simple case of absolute right or wrong; it relates to what the powerful people have decided should be right and wrong and this changes over time. Note that it is not advisable to use too many scare quotes in a piece of academic writing.

3.8 Conclusion: advice about participles

- While Standard English is just a powerful dialect rather than an absolute correct form that lasts for ever, it pays to know how and when to use it. Your use of past participles, such as 'written' and 'done', can still single you out as someone who has a good education or not.
- Present participles end in -ing. If they are being used as part of a description of another part of the sentence, they must be properly related to that part of the sentence.
- Past participles are often irregular. Regular ones are the same as the past tense, thus I have walked/I walked. Some dialects use irregular past tense and past participle interchangeably.
- Present and past participles are incomplete forms of the verb. The next chapter looks at how to make them complete. The participles are used to form different tenses; they need other verbs to help them though.

3.8.1 Technical terms relating to this chapter

For further information, look up these words in the Glossary, other grammar books or the World Wide Web.

Auxiliary verbs (explained in next chapter)
Dangling participle
Dialect
Finite verbs
Misrelated participle
Past participle
Perfect tense (explained in next chapter)
Present participle
Scare quotes
Standard English

4

Getting tense with verbs

- *What's going on – or was going on?*
- *Should you write in the past or present?*

Many students get into difficulties when they are writing about events that
have happened in the past, but still have implications for the present. Barbara's
dilemma, presented below, may be familiar to anyone who has had to write
about the ideas of the ancient Greeks (and other long-dead authors).

4.1 Barbara's dilemma: here and now – or there and then?

Abel has arrived first at the café as Barbara has stopped to pick up her essay.
He's skimming through a chapter of a book that he needs for his tutorial. He is
soon interrupted when Barbara does arrive; she's obviously in a bad mood. She

flings her essay on the table. Abel looks at the cover. The mark's not too bad, but there is a single comment on it – *Tenses!*

Barbara: What's that supposed to mean? Is it good, or bad – or what?
Abel: 'Tenses' means past and present and future. Maybe you've used the wrong one. Give me a look.
Barbara: Well, I don't know what he's talking about. See if you can work it out and I'll get myself a drink.

Abel looks at the essay, takes out a pencil and lightly underlines each verb in the first paragraph. Barbara comes back with a cappuccino.

Barbara: Hey – what are you doing?
Abel: I'm finding it confusing too, so I thought I'd underline the verbs and see if I could work it out. Look, this bit's future, this is in the present – and I'm not sure what this is supposed to be!
Barbara: Well perhaps it should all be in the past. Plato has been dead for quite some time!
Abel: Yes, but his writing is still here. And I think sometimes you see that and sometimes you don't. And that's when you get things mixed up.
Barbara: I suppose if I'm talking about his ideas, they still sort of exist because they're still being discussed. But when Plato's writing about what Socrates did, shouldn't that be in the past? And it's kind of hard to separate the ideas from what Socrates did. So should I say 'Socrates said . . .' or 'Socrates says . . .' I mean, Socrates didn't write anything, so all that's left of him is what Plato says about him.
Abel: Plato *says* – that's present.
Barbara: Yes, that's what I would actually say – but can I write it in an essay as well? I do think Plato's still saying something, even though he's dead and the events are in the past.
Abel: And there are different types of event, whether it's present, past or future. There are things that happen, things that happen at a particular time, and things that happen during a period of time. And you have to think about whether the event's over or is still going on.
Barbara: Whoa, slow down a bit! That's too confusing.

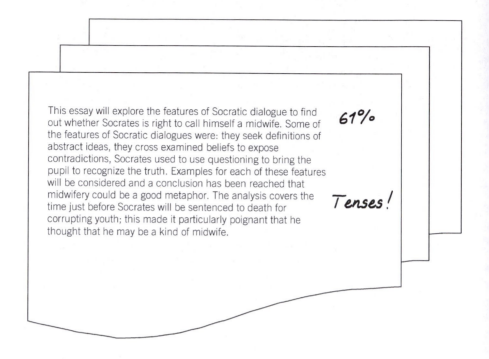

This essay will explore the features of Socratic dialogue to find out whether Socrates is right to call himself a midwife. Some of the features of Socratic dialogues were: they seek definitions of abstract ideas, they cross examined beliefs to expose contradictions, Socrates used to use questioning to bring the pupil to recognize the truth. Examples for each of these features will be considered and a conclusion has been reached that midwifery could be a good metaphor. The analysis covers the time just before Socrates will be sentenced to death for corrupting youth; this made it particularly poignant that he thought that he may be a kind of midwife.

61%

Tenses!

4.1.1 Extract from Barbara's essay with confusing tenses

This essay <u>will explore</u> the features of Socratic dialogue to find out whether Socrates <u>is</u> right to call himself a midwife. Some of the features of Socratic dialogues <u>were:</u> they <u>seek</u> definitions of abstract ideas, they <u>cross-examined</u> beliefs to expose contradictions, Socrates <u>used to use</u> questioning to bring the pupil to recognize the truth. Examples for each of these features <u>will be considered</u> and a conclusion <u>has been reached</u> that midwifery <u>could be</u> a good metaphor. The analysis <u>covers</u> the time just before Socrates <u>will be sentenced</u> to death for corrupting youth; this <u>made</u> it particularly poignant that he <u>thought</u> that he <u>may be</u> a kind of midwife.

4.2 Questions about tenses

1 Do you think that Barbara should write in the present or the past when she's referring to Socratic dialogues?
2 When is it OK to have a mixture of tenses?
3 What are the differences between the following? (Think about how they might be used.)

I have written	I had written	I shall have written
I was writing	I had been writing	I shall be writing
I did write	I would write	I ought to write

Answers to these questions are explored in this chapter and you'll find further comments in Section 4.8.

When Abel underlines the verbs, Barbara can see that she has a mixture of tenses and has not been consistent in her writing. She and Abel agree to see if they can find information in the library and on the internet that will tell them about tenses. They want to produce a list of different uses in the past, present and future. Their combined results are in Figure 4.3.

4.3 How the form of a verb shows its tense

The tense of a verb is the form that shows the time of the action. Some writers say that English verbs only have two main tenses – present and past.

Present
It is Sunday today.
I write letters on a Sunday.

Past
It *was* Saturday yesterday.
I *wrote* a letter yesterday.

Think about what these simple sentences tell us about the **time** and **duration** of the action or condition. Is it still happening? Is it complete?

Present: It is Sunday today – all day. I regularly write letters on a Sunday. In the simple present tense, the action is something that is here and now. The present tense describes an action or condition that is currently the case or regularly happens and is often used for making general statements, for example: 'He writes very well.'
Past: It was Saturday yesterday and that is in the past. I wrote a letter – the action is over.

For the verb 'to write', we only have the forms: write, writes and wrote. There are also incomplete parts of the verb:

the *infinitive*	(to) write
the present participle	writing
the past participle	written

These are used to make up other tenses, but they need some help.

	First person	Second person	Third person
write	I write; we write	you write	they write
writes			he/she/it writes; Plato writes
wrote	I wrote; we wrote	you wrote	he/she/it wrote; Plato wrote; they wrote

FIGURE 4.1 Simple forms of the verb 'write'.

4.4 Auxiliary verbs

We often want to say more with our verbs than express what is current or what has happened and is over. In some cases, we have to add a helping or auxiliary verb to one of the participles – 'writing' or 'written' – or to the infinitive – '(to) write'. That's when it starts to get complicated.

In Figure 4.2, there are examples of forms of the verb 'to write' that relate to past, present and future. For each of these, we consider

- the simple form;
- the continuous form (when it is over a particular period);
- the perfect form (when it is complete);
- the perfect continuous form (when it combines completion and continuity).

These examples are summarized in Figure 4.2, for the active form.

For native English speakers, the main problems occur when students don't stay consistently in one set of tenses, usually the present or past. For non-native speakers, there may not be an exact equivalent to the tenses in their own first language and there are some subtle distinctions of usage.

	Present	Past	Future
Simple	write/s	wrote	will write
Continuous	am/is/are writing	was/were writing	will be writing
Perfect (complete)	have/has written	had written	will have written
Perfect (continuous)	have/has been writing	had been writing	will have been writing

FIGURE 4.2 Summary of past, present and future verb forms.

4.5 Some examples of tenses

Barbara and Abel have made up a chart of examples of present, past and future uses, based on material they found on the internet and in grammar books (see the Bibliography for some suggested sources). Barbara intends to use this as a check for her essays until she gets more used to writing them. She has still to decide whether she wants to write in the present or the past about dead authors, but she wants to get to grips with all the possible tenses first. Their chart is shown in Figure 4.3.

It seems to Barbara that there's an unexpected bonus to being able to think about whether things are complete or continuous . . .

4.6 Barbara's past, present and future

Barbara:	This is all starting to make sense. I see why you could want a past tense to describe something that's over. That guy Mark – he *has been* my boyfriend but definitely isn't now. I see why they talk about 'has-beens' – it means it's definitely in the past and is no longer.
Abel:	But you *have been talking* to me for the past hour and it is still happening – I hope!
Barbara:	Yeah, but there is a difference. He *has been* a boyfriend uses the past of the verb 'to be'. It's complete – look at the chart, it's a present perfect. But he has been *talking* is a different verb – 'to talk'. It's a continuous perfect – it's still going on.
Abel:	Yes, you're right. I like the idea of something being continuous. We were talking, we are talking, we are going to the pub tonight . . .
Barbara:	Who said we're doing that?
Abel:	I shall have finished my essay by the time you take me to the pub tonight – a future perfect. Sounds perfect to me anyway!

But Barbara isn't listening . . .

Barbara:	He is so in the past, that Mark guy. I *went* out with him; I *was going* out with him; I *had gone* out with him before I came to my senses. How far past and over can I make it? Is there anything more past than the pluperfect?

As you can see from the chart in Figure 4.3, the auxiliaries are formed from the verbs 'to be' and 'to have'. Another verb is commonly used in this way: 'to do' (see Figure 4.4). It is particularly useful for expressing emphasis or negatives of the simple present or past. It is also useful for questions.

Examples relating to the present

Example	Tense	Usage
The student **writes** essays well.	Present	This is happening now or happens regularly. It **is** complete.
The student **is writing** the essay now/today.	Continuous present (or can be future)	It may be an action that is currently happening, or it may express intention for the immediate future. This construction suggests that the action happens over a specific period of time and usually refers to visible action.
The student **has written** an excellent essay.	Present perfect	This describes something completed, at an unspecified time. Though the action is in the past, its effect is in the present.
The student **has been writing** an essay.	Continuous perfect	This describes something that began in the past, is still happening and may continue into the future.

Examples relating to the past

Example	Tense	Usage
The student **wrote** an essay last week.	Past	It happened in the past.
The student **was writing** an essay when the fire started.	Continuous past	It happened in the past at the same time as something else.
The student **had written** the essay when the fire started.	Past perfect (*Pluperfect*)	It happened in the past, and was completed before something else.
The student **had been writing** the essay before the fire started.	Continuous past perfect	It began in the past and was ongoing, but was completed before something else.

Examples relating to the future

Example	Tense	Usage
The student **will write** an essay.	Future	It has not happened yet, but will happen in the future.
The student **will be writing** an essay about literacy.	Continuous future	This is continuous action, implying a particular period of time in the future.
The student **will have written** the essay before the tutorial.	Future perfect	It will happen, and be completed before some other future event.
The student **will have been writing** the essay for three months by then.	Future perfect continuous	It will happen, it will be ongoing, it will still be happening at a specified time.

FIGURE 4.3 Examples of tenses and their usage.

The student **does write** essays well.	This use is emphatic, highlighting the word "well". Often this is used to confirm that something is the case, when there may be a doubt.
The student **did write** an essay last week.	
Does the student **write** essays?	These are the same sentences turned into questions.
Did the student **write** the essay?	
The student **does not write** essays well.	This is the conventional way of forming the negative of the present and past tense.
The student **did not write** essays well.	

FIGURE 4.4 Using 'do' as an auxiliary verb.

Barbara is quite pleased with their chart and sets about revising her essay, to help her practise for next time. She makes the following decisions to help her to be consistent.

Barbara's decisions about tenses (note that other decisions would also have been acceptable):

- The essay exists for the reader, so I'm going to write about it in the present tense. So I'll say: 'This essay explores features of Socratic dialogue . . .'
- Socratic dialogue also exists for the reader, so I'll write about that in the present too: 'Some of the features of Socratic dialogue are . . .'
- If I want to write about something that happened at a specific time, I'd better put that in the past: 'Socrates died in 399 BC.'
- So if I'm talking about Socratic dialogue before Socrates died, I have to decide whether I'm writing about an event that is over and in the past or about the ideas that are still there for the reader to see.
- A mixture of tenses will be OK if I'm clear about whether it's an event that's in the past or a theory that can currently be read.

Go to Section 4.8 to see how Barbara rewrote the first paragraph of her essay.

Abel's thoughts are more with the future. He is also starting to think about what *might* be, what *could* be and what *ought* to be. Like Barbara, Abel is thinking about his personal life as well as his academic writing. The examples in Figure 4.5 show what he is thinking about the essay he is currently writing; he has some other thoughts relating to what is possible, necessary and obligatory with respect to (a) going to the pub this evening and (b) his relationship with Barbara!

Example	Usage
I **should write** my own essay.	There is a sense of an obligation.
I **ought to write** the essay now.	This also suggests obligation – rather strongly.
I **would write** the essay if I stopped chatting.	Here there is an idea of a condition – something else has to happen as well.
I **can write** the essay	The student is able to do this.
I **may write** the essay on Newton.	This could express either permission or a possibility – the student is allowed to or it is possible that the student will do it.
I **could write** the essay on Einstein instead.	There is a sense of the student's ability, but also an element of uncertainty.
I **must write** a draft of the essay this afternoon.	'Must' expresses necessity, compulsion or obligation (depending on the context).

FIGURE 4.5 Other auxiliary verbs (*modal auxiliaries*).

This introduces a whole range of other auxiliary verbs – notice the subtle differences that Abel can think about.

Notice that in all of these verbs, the form does not change for the 3rd person (unlike 'he writes the essay', for example). Thus we might say, if it were any of our business:

He should finish the essay today.
He ought to write the essay before going to the pub.
He would write the essay if he stopped thinking about Barbara.
He can write the essay.
He may fall asleep instead of doing the essay.
He could ask Barbara out.
He must phone Barbara before 9.00 pm or she will be out already.

These verbs are unusual ones. If you are interested in finding out more about them, look up 'modal auxiliaries' in a grammar book or on the Web.

Most native English speakers would use these verbs automatically without thinking too much about it. I have mentioned them here to point out that it can be very useful to express levels of ability, certainty, conditions, obligations and necessity. You'll see how useful it is in the final extract from the students' discussions about tenses – how auxiliary verbs can help you to 'hedge' in essays (and other things). *Hedging* means being cautious about claims that you make – which can be important in academic writing, including factual writing. You can hedge using words such as 'possibly' or 'conceivably', or through using particular constructions such as 'It is suggested that . . .'. You can also use some of the auxiliary verbs that Abel has just been considering.

4.7 Facts and possibilities – using the appropriate tense

Barbara and Kim get to the pub first, but Abel has promised to join them when he has written 500 words. Barbara tells Kim about their progress with tenses and shows her the chart in Figure 4.2. Because Kim is studying engineering, she has a different perspective.

Kim:	What this? An instruction for a time machine?
Barbara:	It's amazing how many tenses there are – ways of expressing different types of time.
Kim:	So you've made up a time chart. I wouldn't bother with a lot of that stuff – I just have to give the facts in my writing for uni. And usually it's a report about something that was done, so I keep it in the past.
Barbara:	What about quoting from other writers? Or talking about theories?
Kim:	Well, I suppose that some things are always true – such as Newton's second law of motion. I'd probably write that in the present tense. Perhaps your time machine chart might be useful. *[Sings]* Let's do the time warp again . . . *[Barbara gives her a funny look.]*
Barbara:	I think Abel's writing about Newton.
Kim:	Yeah, but he's doing it from a historical perspective – he's probably writing about events in the past.
Barbara:	He's analysing Newton's ideas though, so that could be present. Look, here he is now, just in time to get a round in.

Abel looks as though he has a few things on his mind – he does. As well as thinking about Newton, he has an awkward question to ask Barbara. But he's been reading about 'hedging' – using auxiliary verbs that express possibility rather than fact or necessity.

Barbara:	Hi Abel – we're talking about tenses. Are you writing about Newton in the past or the present?
Abel:	A bit of both – when it's a fact about his life, it's past.
Kim:	But his ideas have become facts too, haven't they?
Abel:	Well, I do use the present when I'm talking about his ideas, but I have to watch what I'm claiming to be 'fact'. I find I'm using a lot of hedging.
Barbara:	You're supposed to be writing an essay, not gardening!
Abel:	No – I'm toning things down a bit. Making sure I don't overstate my case. And I'm using some other auxiliary verbs, especially when I'm adding my own interpretations. So I'm saying things like 'Newton could have intended . . .' (because I don't know what he actually

intended) or 'Newton seems to be suggesting . . .'. Words like may, might, could or would are very useful for avoiding sounding like a know-all.

Kim: I use 'it' to do this as well – like, 'it may be the case that . . .', 'it could be interpreted as. . . .'

Abel: That makes it even more distant.

Kim: In technical subjects, though some things are facts, you do have to be careful not to make strong claims that might not actually be the case. We have to do quite a bit of hedging. You see it in the books we're reading too.

Barbara: But if you overdo the hedging, then you end up not saying anything. All these mights and maybes – don't you lose the point?

Kim: Yeah, when I'm checking I take out some of my vague stuff if I know I can be very definite. But if I find I'm giving a strong opinion, like, 'This result means that our whole life changes' then I usually try and soften it in some way – like, 'it could have a major impact on our lives'.

Barbara: So you have to avoid being too definite, even with facts.

Kim: Sometimes.

Abel: Barbara, I was wondering . . .

Barbara: Yeah?

Abel: Could you. . ., would you . . .?

Kim [laughs]: She may, she might, she should!

Barbara: Shut up Kim. What is it Abel?

Abel: Barbara – could you lend me a tenner so I can get a round in?

4.8 Comments on questions

1 Do you think that Barbara should write in the present or the past when she's referring to Socratic dialogues?

Neither would be wrong. This chapter suggests that it is useful to think of the dialogues as texts that continue to exist and to write about them in the present. However, it would be perfectly acceptable to regard them as past events and to write about them in the past. It is important to be consistent – decide whether you're using the present or past when referring to writers. The present is rather more manageable, especially when it is necessary to refer to previous events.

2 When is it OK to have a mixture of tenses?

Even when you are writing in the present, it is sometimes necessary to indicate that an event is completely in the past – especially if there is a specific time associated with it. An example of this is that Socrates died in 399 BC. It is also sometimes necessary to indicate that one event preceded – or will precede – another, in which case a mixture of tenses is necessary.

3 What are the differences between the following? (Think about how they might be used.)

I have written	I had written	I shall have written
I was writing	I had been writing	I shall be writing
I did write	I would write	I ought to write

Each of the first two rows is used to express a different time – present, past or future and a level of completion. In the third row, there are other ideas being suggested. Thus:

I have written – this is past and complete, but the effect is still present.
I had written – this is definitely past and complete and happened before something else.
I shall have written – this has not happened yet, but something else will be happening after it.

I was writing – this is past and continuous.
I had been writing – this is past, continuous and complete (before something else).
I shall be writing – this is future and continuous, over a period of (unspecified) time.

I did write – this is past, emphasizing what I did (possibly someone has denied it).
I would write – this suggests a condition has to be met first.
I ought to write – there is an obligation here.

4.8.1 Barbara's revision to her essay

This essay *explores* the features of Socratic dialogue to find out whether Socrates *was* right to call himself a midwife. Some of the features of Socratic dialogues *are*: they *seek* definitions of abstract ideas, they *cross-examine* beliefs to expose contradictions, Socrates *uses* questioning to bring the pupil to recognize the truth. Examples for each of these features *are considered* and it *is concluded* that midwifery *could be* a good metaphor. The analysis *covers* the time just before

Socrates *was sentenced* to death for corrupting youth; this *makes* it particularly poignant that he *thinks* that he *may be* a kind of midwife.

Because she is moving between past and present, Barbara decides that it might be helpful to find alternative ways of expressing some of the verbs she is using.

4.8.2 Alternative expression, reducing the number of finite verbs

This essay *explores* the features of Socratic dialogue to assess the accuracy of Socrates's description of himself as a midwife. Particular attention *is paid* to Socrates's attempts to seek definitions of abstract ideas, to cross-examine beliefs to expose contradictions, and to use questioning to bring the pupil to recognize the truth. These features *suggest* that midwifery *could be* a good metaphor. The analysis *covers* the time just before Socrates' death sentence for corrupting youth; his idea that he *is* a kind of midwife *is* therefore particularly poignant.

4.9 Conclusion: advice about tenses

- Decide which tense you are writing in and stick to it.
- A mixture of tenses may still be acceptable, but there should be a reason for it.
- If you are puzzled about the tense to use, think about whether the action should be continuous or complete (or both).
- If you think you are making over-strong statements, consider using tenses that suggest possibility rather than necessity.
- When you are checking an assignment, check for consistency.

4.9.1 Technical terms relating to this chapter

For further information, look up these words in the Glossary, other grammar books or the World Wide Web.

Auxiliary verbs
Finite verbs
Hedging
Infinitive
Modal auxiliaries
Participles (see Chapter 3)
Perfect tense
Person
Pluperfect
Tense

5

Active and passive voices

5.1 Abel gives voice to his frustrations • 5.2 Questions about the passive voice • 5.3 Reasons for using the passive • 5.4 When passives get awkward • 5.5 When Kim gets awkward • 5.6 Comments on questions • 5.7 Conclusion: advice about the passive voice

- *What's the difference between active and passive?*
- *How can you write in an impersonal way?*

5.1 Abel gives voice to his frustrations

Barbara has invited the others round to her flat as Abel's computer has broken. Abel has been running his latest essay through the grammar checker on Barbara's computer. When he gets to the sentence, 'Galileo was considered to be a heretic and was brought to trial by the Inquisition' the checker announces, 'There appears to be a verb in the *passive voice*.' Abel starts shouting at the computer.

Abel: Speak English, why don't you! What's passive?
Kim: The passive's OK – I use it all the time in my reports. It saves me having to say 'I'. So instead of saying, 'I calibrated the micrometer'

	I say, 'The micrometer was calibrated'. It gets rid of me altogether – some people might think that's a good idea!
Abel:	Is that why they call it voice? You've got no voice – no real say in what you're writing? That's what it feels like to me; we get it in science too – if I calibrate it, why shouldn't I say so? But I wasn't avoiding 'I' here anyway.
Barbara:	I suppose it is about whose voice you're hearing. In your sentence, you could have said the Inquisition considered Galileo a heretic and brought him to trial. Then you'd have been hearing the Inquisition's voice – well, at least getting the sentence more from their point of view.
Abel:	But I wanted to emphasize Galileo and what was done to him.
Kim:	Think about that, though – it's a good way of putting it. You use the passive when you want to emphasize what happens to something or someone. And you use the active when you want to emphasize what something or someone does.
Barbara:	So active's like, 'I hate that guy Mark' and passive's, 'That guy is hated.' Well hated, in fact and not just by me! So I'd use the passive if I wanted to say more about him than me.
Abel:	That makes sense. But I don't think you should say any more about him anyway. *[Quickly moving on]* I got pulled up for saying, 'I have found no scientific evidence' when it was the evidence, or lack of it, that I wanted to highlight. So, 'No scientific evidence was found' would be better – and it takes me out of the picture.
Barbara:	What about, 'There is no scientific evidence'? Wouldn't that be better?
Kim:	Well, it would be OK if you could say for certain that Abel's looked at all the possible evidence. The speed he's working at just now, I don't think that's likely.
Abel:	That sounds like a sneer, Kim.
Kim:	But not a grammar one. Actually, I think you're right to say, 'No scientific evidence was found.'
Barbara:	Well, I still think mine's better – 'There is no scientific evidence . . .'

5.2 Questions about the passive voice

1 How can you tell the difference between the active and the passive?
2 Why do some grammar checkers object to the passive while some lecturers love it?

3 Which is the better impersonal version of 'I have found no scientific evidence . . .' – Abel's version or Barbara's?

5.3 Reasons for using the passive

Grammar books report the following reasons for using the passive voice: to emphasize what was done to something or someone; to be impersonal; to avoid giving a person's identity (either because it is unknown or inappropriate).

In each case in Figure 5.1, further information might be available by adding an expression (after the verb) beginning with the word 'by': 'by the Athenian Assembly'; 'by the author'; 'by the British Navy'. When this happens, it actually counteracts the original reasons for using the passive – it highlights the identity of the people who did the action. So it is possible to use the passive to draw attention to an individual agent, as well as to avoid doing this.

The passive is often used in official writing or speech. 'Customers are requested not to smoke.' 'Passengers are reminded that passports are required.' This avoids having to say who is requesting, reminding or requiring.

Grammar books also suggest that you should avoid the use of the passive if possible. The active is more direct and easier to read. There are ways of making even neutral academic writing more active. To take the example of the literature review in Figure 5.1, here are some alternative approaches, still neutral but using the active voice:

Active but impersonal:

- The literature on social policy provides some useful background to this issue.
- A review of literature on social policy follows this introduction.
- The first stage of the project has involved a review of literature on social policy.

Reason for using passive	Example
To emphasize what was done to something/someone	Socrates was accused of corruption.
To be impersonal	The literature has been reviewed for information on social policy.
To avoid giving a person's identity	The ship was torpedoed during the war.

FIGURE 5.1 Reasons for using the passive, with examples.

In the first and second examples, it is obvious that the author has made a review of the literature and just wants to get on and say why it was important. In the third one, the author is keen to specify that he or she has completed a literature review.

5.4 When passives get awkward

The passive is usually formed with part of the verb 'to be' and the past participle.

> The dog ate the bone. (Active)
> The bone *was eaten*. (Passive)

> The dog is eating the bone. (Active)
> The bone *is being eaten*. (Passive)

You can find passives in almost any tense, but there are some cases where rewriting would be preferable. For example, you can interchange the following sentences:

> The student writes essays well. (Active)
> The essays *are well* written. (Passive)

However, if you try to change 'The student has been writing an essay' to the passive, it gets a bit messy. 'An essay has been being written' doesn't sound right at all. You might want to say something like: 'An essay has been started.'
   Some verbs do not translate well into the passive voice. Think of Martin Luther King's famous statement:

> I have a dream. (Active)

'A dream is had' just wouldn't sound idiomatic. If Martin Luther King had not wanted to use the first person, he might have used an expression such as:

> There is a dream. (Passive)

(It would have worked grammatically, but would definitely not have been so powerful!)
   The following example shows another type of problem:

> I have tried to give evidence for my main findings. (Active)

You certainly might want to make this passive to get rid of the 'I'. But you don't want the findings to 'have been tried to be given'! It would be better to say:

An attempt has been made to give evidence for the main findings. (Passive)

You should always remember that there are other possible ways of writing anything. Rather than tie yourself in knots trying to turn an 'I' expression into a passive, you might find a better way of putting it. For example, the passive example above might be better as:

Where possible, the report contains the evidence for the main findings. (Active, but impersonal)

5.5 When Kim gets awkward

All this talk about the passive voice has made Kim feel rather active. She has been looking through one of her engineering books and has found that it uses the passive voice throughout.

Kim: Look at this – the body is constrained, the table is shown, the forces are applied, the transformation has been described . . . no wonder I've found it all so hard to follow.

Barbara: It's just as bad in philosophy – ideas are derived, causes are attributed, identity is postulated . . .

Kim: Well, you'd expect philosophy to be vague, but science and engineering should be precise. So it should say who or what is doing the constraining or applying the forces. I think I'm going to use active verbs right throughout my own project.

Abel: But it won't be neutral enough if you do. You can't just start shoving 'I' in – the engineers hate it.

Kim: No, but it must be possible to write things in plain English.

Barbara: I don't think philosophy's vague – it's trying to be precise too.

Kim: And when I do my presentation, I'll use a lot of active verbs for that. It's OK to use 'I' and 'we' in presentations. And the active verbs will be much better for speech.

Barbara: I think I'm too passive myself – I just let things be done to me, instead of being the person who's doing things.

Kim: Well go and do something useful, like get us the biscuits. I've got a talk to write. An active one.

5.6 Comments on questions

1 How can you tell the difference between the active and the passive?

You are looking at the action in the sentence. Where is the emphasis? Is it on what someone or something is doing (active)? Or is the emphasis on what is done to them?

    Active   The students gave a presentation.
    Passive   The students were given a standing ovation.

The passive is usually formed with a part of the verb 'to be' and the past participle.

2 Why do some grammar checkers object to the passive while some lecturers love it?

The passive voice is more difficult to follow. People often criticize it for hiding the identity of the person who is doing the action. Some lecturers like the passive voice, however, because it encourages neutral language, especially avoiding 'I'. It focuses on what has been done rather than on who did it.

3 Which is the better impersonal version of 'I have found no scientific evidence . . .' – Abel's version or Barbara's?

'There is' or 'there are' are useful expressions if you want to be impersonal: for example, 'There are several possible ways to explore this topic.'

   In this example, however, Barbara's claim that 'There is no scientific evidence' is a very strong one. An experienced lecturer who has read the main works on a topic might be able to make such a claim (and they frequently do); Abel is probably safer just to say that 'No scientific evidence was found', or he could hedge and say: 'There is apparently no scientific evidence . . .'.

5.7 Conclusion: advice about the passive voice

- The passive is formed from a form of the verb 'to be' along with the past participle, for example: 'The problem *is described* below.'
- It is particularly used in neutral impersonal writing and where the emphasis is on what is done to the subject rather than on the person or thing doing it (the agent).

- Don't feel that you have to change your sentence just because the grammar checker says it's passive.
- However, it is sometimes worth asking whether active verbs would be preferable.
- It's not always necessary to do a straight translation between active and passive; often there is a better way of saying the same thing.

5.7.1 Technical terms relating to this chapter

For further information, look up these words in the Glossary, other grammar books or the World Wide Web.

Active voice
Passive
Voice

6

What is the subject?

- *Who or what is doing things?*
- *Who or what is having things done to them?*

Barbara is amazed at how much discussions about grammar seem to be relevant for her personal life. She has put the guy, Mark, from last semester into the past tense. She thinks perhaps she needs to be more active rather than

It is important to be clear about the physical and
other relationships between cause and effect. One
example frequently given is the cause of a car
stopping at a traffic light. This is different from the
previous example with the billiard ball. The traffic
light is not the mechanical link between cause and
effect. Though indirectly causes the car to stop. This
means that we need to consider not

*No
subject!*

passive; she should do something rather than let it happen to her. In this chapter, we find out how being a subject of a sentence relates to doing things or having things done to you. Subjects can be people, things or ideas. The subject is usually the topic of a sentence; the action of the sentence happens in relation to the subject.

6.1 Barbara's favourite subject

Barbara's next problem comes when her lecturer, who seems to like making terse comments, writes 'No subject!' in the margin of her essay. Barbara is annoyed; she thinks that he means that she hasn't followed the topic. She bumps into Kim and persuades her to have a look at the comment.

Barbara: When I think of the time I spent making sure I understood the question! Of course there's a subject here: the subject's cause and effect.

Kim: No he doesn't mean the subject of the essay – he's only underlined one sentence. I think you can talk about the subject of a sentence. Where's your dictionary? Look up 'subject' and see if there's anything with 'gram' with the definition. That means it's about grammar.

[Barbara always carries her dictionary around with her – though her shoulder hurts because it is so heavy!]

Barbara: Oh yes – here we go. *[Reads]* 'That part of a sentence or *clause* denoting the person or thing about which something is said (*gram*).'

Kim: So what should it be? For the bit he's underlined, you've just written, 'Though indirectly causes the car to stop.' What do you mean? What causes the car to stop?

Barbara: It's in the sentence before – it's a traffic light. I don't want to keep repeating myself.

Kim: You still need something to do the causing, even if it's just 'it'. Perhaps this belongs to the previous sentence anyway, because 'though' creates a link. So it should be, 'The traffic light is not the mechanical link between cause and effect, though it indirectly causes the car to stop.' Then the subject of 'is' is 'traffic light' and the subject of 'causes' is 'it'.

Barbara: D'you know, I think I'd have noticed that if I had read it over. I was late finishing it. It doesn't sound right, does it? 'Though indirectly

> causes the car to stop.' If I'd spent time checking it, I'd have wondered what that meant.
>
> *Kim:* I've starting reading stuff aloud now. It's amazing what you pick up. And I know I've picked up that kind of problem before, but I didn't know it was called the subject of the sentence.
>
> *Barbara:* So the subject is what does the action. Or I suppose it could have the action done to it – like when it's passive. A bit like me. Barbara chooses terrible men. That's when I'm being active. Barbara is chosen by terrible men. That's when I'm passive and it's even worse.
>
> *Kim:* That's a good example. Someone has to do the choosing or be chosen. So Barbara is the subject of the sentence in both cases.
>
> *Barbara:* Why don't they teach you that at school? I like being a subject.
>
> *Kim:* I've noticed!

6.2 Questions about subjects of sentences

Richard Palmer in *The Good Grammar Guide* (2003:183) defines 'subject' as: 'The agent in a sentence – i.e. whoever or whatever is "in charge" of the verb.'

1 Look at a paragraph in a book (e.g. the first paragraph of this chapter). Can you identify the main subject of each sentence in that paragraph?
2 Are there ever sentences without subjects?
3 Can there be more than one subject in a sentence?

6.3 Simple and compound subjects

The subject is likely to be a noun or pronoun. It might also be a phrase containing a noun or pronoun. The main subject of a sentence is also likely to come near the beginning of the sentence.

Every sentence (almost – we look briefly at exceptions later) should have a subject and a complete verb. This may be all that the sentence has:

Subject	*Verb*
Barbara	works.
I	have finished.
Ideas	will change.

These are rather short sentences and too many of them together would make the writing jerky and stilted. The main point is that if there is not a verb and a subject for that verb, then it is probably not a sentence. There are some exceptions. For example, 'Please shut the gate.' would be regarded as a sentence, though the subject (you) is not explicit. The exceptions are unusual, however, and it is useful for you to keep reminding yourself that you need a verb and someone or something in charge of it.

There is more detail about what a sentence is in Chapter 7. To help us to build up to that, we need to think some more about subjects and, especially, what can go wrong with them.

The first point to notice is that the subject and the verb should match – or *agree*, as the grammar books say.

I work.
Barbara works.
He works.
They work.

Sentences can contain more than one subject; in fact, it is easy to combine the sentences above using a *compound subject*.

Barbara and I work.
Barbara and he work.

Then the verb has to be a plural one because the subject is plural.

6.4 When subjects move around

When the sentences are short like those we've just considered, it is unlikely that you will get the *agreement* wrong. But look at the following examples.

Barbara, despite spending a lot of time thinking about both Mark and Abel, **works** extensively in the early mornings.
I – the author of this book about grammar – **work** at a Scottish University.

In cases like this, the verb becomes separated from the subject. This is because an extra group of words has been added as further description for the subject. (Notice how commas or *dashes* separate off this aside; we return to this in Chapter 9.) The danger here is that in the separation, the writer forgets what the subject is and puts the wrong ending in for the verb. There is also a danger if the subject and verb are too far apart that the reader forgets who or what the sentence is about. Both of the sample sentences above run this risk.

Note that if you removed 'I' from the aforementioned second example, you would need to change the verb. The subject then becomes 'The author' rather than 'I'.

The author of this book about grammar **works** at a Scottish University.

Sometimes, there is an expression in front of the subject.

As we are both more alert in the mornings, *Barbara*, who is a fictional character, *and I*, her author, **work** in similar ways.

Here the verb has to be a plural one to take account of the two subjects.

The verb 'to be', as so often happens, has some interesting features. Consider the following expressions.

I was tired.
Barbara is a fictional character.

The words after the verb are known as the complement, because they complete the verb. The sentence could meaningfully (though not elegantly) be reversed – Tired was I. This is not the case with many verbs which have more of a sense of action (rather than just being): try reversing 'The dog ate the bone', for example. In that case, the meaning changes and, indeed, becomes impossible.

Other expressions that are common with the verb 'to be' are:

It is . . .
There is . . .
There are . . .
Are there . . .?

These constructions allow for subjects to be in a different place in the sentence, either for emphasis or for effect. In the following expression, the *adverb* 'there' doesn't really have any meaning of its own, but it allows an impersonal way of introducing 'a price' which is effectively the subject of the sentence.

There is a price to pay for expecting so much from students.

In the case of Jane Austen's famous sentence in *Pride and Prejudice*, the pronoun 'it' is the subject, but it serves to highlight the complement 'a truth':

It is a truth universally acknowledged, that a single man in possession of a good fortune, must be in want of a wife.

Don't worry about the finer details of the above explanation: you probably don't need to know what a complement is anyway. I have just introduced you to the idea so that you are not worried about using such expressions as 'it is' or 'there are'. If you are interested in finding out more about complements, Palmer (2003) has some useful points.

6.5 Subject closed

Barbara and Kim have spent more time thinking about subjects than they intended. Barbara has decided that she's been getting too worked up about grammar.

Barbara: There's less to this than meets the eye. So really, all I had to do was make sure there was something or someone that the sentence was about.
Kim: Looks like it.
Barbara: There's a theme coming out here. What am I trying to say? What's going on? Who or what's doing it? Who or what's having it done to them? And why aren't the interesting answers to that question happening to me?
Kim: Your day will come. Perhaps you'll meet someone at my party. Then you can change the subject.

6.6 Comments on questions

1 Look at a paragraph in a book (e.g. the first paragraph of this chapter). Can you identify the main subject of each sentence in that paragraph?

The main subject of each sentence from the first paragraph of this chapter is italicized. The last sentence is really two sentences joined with a semicolon; this is a topic we'll return to in Chapter 7.

Barbara is amazed at how much discussions about grammar seem to be relevant for her personal life. *She* has put the guy, Mark, from last semester into the past tense. *She* thinks perhaps she needs to be more active rather than passive, just allowing things to be done to her. In this chapter, *we* find out how being a subject of a sentence relates to doing things or having things done to you. *Subjects* can be people, things or ideas. *The subject* is usually the topic of a sentence; *the action of the sentence* happens in relation to the subject.

2 Are there ever sentences without subjects?

It is probably a useful rule of thumb to say that a subject is an essential part of a sentence. However, examples can be found of apparently subjectless sentences – often with implicit subjects as in instructions. 'Shut the door.' is a sentence and the subject is 'you'. 'It is snowing.' is a sentence, but what does it mean to say 'it' is the subject? It certainly does not help if we see a subject as being a topic of a sentence, which is why it is useful to think about grammar and punctuation as well as content for sentences. The main point is that if you are reading over your own writing and it sounds odd, it is always worth checking whether your sentence has a subject or not.

3 Can there be more than one subject in a sentence?

Subjects can be compound, meaning that there is more than one. There are also separate subjects in clauses that are not the main clause in the sentence (we have not yet looked at this, so don't worry if you did not realize it). Finally, as in the last sentence of the first paragraph of this chapter, sometimes sentences are joined together with a word like 'and' or a semicolon. These sentences will have two main clauses and therefore two subjects.

6.7 Conclusion: advice about sentences and subjects

If something you've written doesn't sound right, ask yourself the following questions:

- Does this sentence have at least one subject?
- Is it clear which subject goes with which verb?
- Are the subject and verb so far apart that their connection is lost?
- Do the subject and verb agree (are they both either singular or plural)?

6.7.1 Technical terms relating to this chapter

For further information, look up these words in the Glossary, other grammar books or the World Wide Web.

Agreement
Complement
Compound subject
Subject

7

The complete sentence

- *What is a sentence?*
- *Is there a subject, verb, object?*
- *What gives you a clue that your sentences might be wrong?*
- *How do sentences work together?*

Falling standards, dumbing down, poor literacy levels: journalists seem to have a lot to say about grammar and language, especially when they are talking about younger people. Our students have picked up a newspaper article that complains about the inability of undergraduates to write in sentences. It seems to them to be the worst form of sneering. But is it true?

7.1 Can students write in sentences?

Abel and Barbara are meeting early to discuss a surprise birthday present for Kim. Abel is reading the paper while he waits for Barbara; she arrives just as he is flinging the paper on the floor. Her bag is getting even heavier; as well as her dictionary, she now has a large book from the library: *The Cambridge Encyclopaedia of Language*. The library's edition comes from 1987. (The full reference is in the Bibliography at the end of this book.)

Barbara: What's up?
Abel: That journalist. Spoonfeeding in schools, he says. Illiteracy. Students can't write in sentences. Employers complaining about standards. How biased is that?
Barbara: I suppose when I missed out the subject in my essay, I wasn't writing a proper sentence. But that doesn't mean I can't – I just didn't check it properly.
Abel: I know – they say you can't do something, just 'cause you get it wrong once. That makes me mad.
Barbara: Sorry I'm a bit late, Abel. I was getting this book from the library . . .
Abel: Oh, good. Let's see what it says about sentences.

They use the index and eventually find a section on Page 94.

Barbara: Oh my goodness, it says there are over 200 definitions of what a sentence is. Well, if we're going to get indignant about newspaper articles, we'll need something a bit more definite than that to defend our case.
Abel: 200 definitions of a sentence! How come?
Barbara: [*Skimming the passage*] Well, it could be to do with a thought, the logic, the grammar, the punctuation, the intonation . . . though I suppose we could rule out some because we're thinking about writing, not speech.
Abel: That's not true, though. Kim's particularly worried about grammar for doing her speech.
Barbara: She's also worried about punctuation. Are we going to get her a book on punctuation, by the way?
Abel: Doesn't sound like a twenty-first birthday present.
Barbara: Well, with other things. Things you can eat, drink, listen to or have a bath in. And we'll look for a jokey book, a friendly one. But not a sneery one. Anyway, she's just coming so shut up about presents.

Kim joins them.

Kim: You two look very cosy. What are you plotting?
Barbara: Nothing, we're talking about sentences. What do you think a sentence is?
Kim: Something that starts with a capital letter and ends in a full stop and gives me a nightmare in between.

Barbara:	I think it's more to do with subjects and verbs.
Abel:	Complete verbs – not just bits of them. Not just participles – you know, your favourites Kim.
Kim:	Well I've got my past participles sorted out now, but I still don't know where to put that full stop. And I also don't know how many sentences you should have before you put a space in.
Abel:	From participles to paragraphs. Got a nice ring to it. Participles, sentences, paragraphs – I suppose they're all building blocks we're putting in place.

7.2 Questions about sentences

1 How would you define (a) a sentence and (b) a paragraph?
2 What are the main things that go wrong with sentences – either your own or other people's?

7.3 The sentence as a unit of thought or grammatical structure

A number of definitions of 'sentence' refer to a complete thought or a group of words that make complete grammatical sense. Note that a sentence doesn't have to be true or even make actual sense. Consider: 'The cat has green whiskers.' This is a perfectly acceptable sentence, even if there are no such cats. 'All tulips like gorgonzola.' That's a sentence too, even though it doesn't make much sense at all. It makes grammatical sense: we can follow the structure of it. It helps our understanding to use sensible sentences, however, so we'll start with a few simple ones and then look at some from books.

Some books (for example, Peck and Coyle 1999) refer to the common structure: subject – verb – object. Here are some examples.

Subject	*Verb*	*Object*
Kim	plays	the saxophone.
The idea	worried	anthropologists.
The competition	will not have	a second prize.

This is a useful starting point; we have already seen the importance of the subject and the verb. The object is the receiver of the action. A verb like 'play' might either take an object or not: 'They were only playing.' is a sentence without an object. Some verbs don't usually make sense without an object though – for example, 'take' or 'have' or 'want'. In these cases, the subject takes or has or wants *something*.

Peck and Coyle (1999) say that this basic structure frequently helps students to sort out their writing problems. A quick check that each sentence has a subject and verb – and an object if it needs one – usually helps even experienced writers to write more clearly. Of course, the sentences that experienced writers use do get more complicated. In fact, they're not just complicated: they're also *compound* or *complex*.

> **Question:** Why should we be bothered to learn about compound and complex sentences?
> **Answer:** It should help you with two of the basic problems with sentences – cutting them in half or running them together. But you might not need to worry too much about the terms 'compound' and 'complex'.

7.3.1 Compound sentence

A compound sentence is two or more simple sentences joined together (Figure 7.1).

We saw the word 'compound' in the last chapter – compound subjects are when there are two or more subjects for the same verb. It is the same idea with sentences. When two simple sentences are brought together with a joining word such as 'and' or 'but' they make a compound sentence.

> *Simple sentences*
> Barbara likes chocolate.
> She plans to buy some for Kim.
>
> *Compound sentences*
> Barbara likes chocolate and she plans to buy some for Kim.
> Barbara likes chocolate so she plans to buy some for Kim.

FIGURE 7.1 Turning simple sentences into compound ones.

A word that joins simple sentences to make them compound sentences is known as a conjunction, which means 'connection' or 'union'. Figure 7.2 suggests some that you can use to connect simple sentences of equal value.

> and but
> for or
> nor so
> yet

FIGURE 7.2 Examples of conjunctions that connect simple sentences.

Note that conjunctions can also be used to connect smaller units than sentences, for example in compound subjects as we saw in the last chapter: 'Barbara and Abel are buying a present for Kim.' We can now think about compound objects too: 'Abel will buy coffee and cakes.'

Compound sentences are similarly joining two or more units of equal value. The finite verbs are italicized in the examples below, which are joined by 'but' and 'for' respectively:

Barbara *will buy* chocolate but Abel *has bought* cakes already.
Barbara *is not buying* it today for she *might eat* it herself.

7.3.2 Complex sentence

A complex sentence is a simple sentence (or main clause) with at least one *dependent clause*.

A clause is a group of words with a subject and a finite verb. I have already suggested that this is a possible definition of a sentence – and, in fact, another way of describing a sentence is to say that it contains a principal or main clause. Sometimes, however, another clause is added to the main one with a joining word that makes it dependent on the main clause.

There are also conjunctions to join parts of complex sentences. Examples of such conjunctions can be seen in Figure 7.3.

If you see one of the words in Figure 7.3, you can tell that there is a dependent clause in the sentence. It depends on the main clause to make sense. It is perhaps easier to understand the idea of a dependent clause through examples. The italicized bits in the examples below are all dependent clauses that link to the main clause through a conjunction. They can't stand by themselves because they have this joining word.

Although Barbara likes chocolate, she will give it away to Kim.
Because Barbara likes chocolate, she thinks Kim will like it too.
If Kim likes chocolate, Barbara will buy it for her birthday.

after	although
as	because
before	how
if	once
since	than
that	though
till	unless
until	when
where	whether
while	

FIGURE 7.3 Examples of conjunctions that connect parts of complex sentences.

If you just saw the expression 'because Barbara likes chocolate', you would think it was incomplete. It is dependent on another clause to explain what the connection is that 'because' is making. Sometimes people use incomplete sentences for effect, so you will occasionally see them. But it is better not to do this if you don't understand why it's creating a good effect.

By the way, if anyone ever tells you not to start a sentence with 'because', show them the aforementioned second example, which is correct according to Standard English. In this sequence, it stresses the reason that Barbara thinks Kim will like chocolate (in this case, drawing attention to the fact that it's not a particularly good reason!). It's rather more common to see a 'because' statement after the main clause, for example: 'Barbara has bought chocolate because Abel says he likes it.' It is certainly not incorrect to do it, but so many teachers have told students that they should never start a sentence with 'because' that it might be safer not to! All you need to do is reverse the sequence so that the main clause comes first.

It is useful to think about the type of dependent clause you are using. In the three examples shown earlier:

1   'Although' is a conjunction that shows concession – even if something is the case, an action will happen that might not be expected. Other examples are 'though' and 'even if'.
2   'Because' is a conjunction that shows the cause for the action. Other examples are 'as' and 'since'.
3   'If' is a conjunction that shows the conditions that will make the action happen. Other examples are 'whether' and 'unless'.

There are other frequently used conjunctions, particularly to do with time and place, for example: 'after', 'since', 'when', 'where'.

Question: Why do we need to know about conjunctions?

Answer: These words are extremely useful for making sentences sound more sophisticated and also for showing where your argument might be going.

Think of the useful questions to ask yourself about your main verb: **where, why, how** and **when**. If you can answer any of these, you might have a useful dependent clause; for example: 'Barbara will buy chocolate when she has some money.' **Who** and **which** are other interesting questions – used with nouns rather than verbs – and we'll come back to them in the next chapter where there is some more to say about dependent clauses.

The sentence, then, may be a unit of thought or a logical relationship between subject, verb and object and it may also benefit from some elaboration. These are quite tricky points; it is worth looking at them in relation to some real pieces of writing. Grammar books, including this one, often use over-simplified sentences as illustrations. Then when you look at real life stuff, it doesn't seem to have any relationship to the examples.

Figure 7.4 contains two extracts: one from an engineering book and one from a philosophy book. In each case, I have underlined the subject and emboldened the verb in the main clause of the sentence. Here are some comments on how understanding the grammatical sense can sometimes help the reader to understand the actual sense.

Let's look at each example sentence by sentence, identifying subject, verb and object (where available). I have tried to pare each sentence back to the minimum statement of these; the comments show that this approach has limitations and raises additional issues. Nevertheless, looking for the basic structure – subject, verb, object – is a useful way of getting to the heart of what is going on. Figure 7.5 shows this analysis with Example 1 and Figure 7.6

Subjects and Verbs: Example 1

A branch of analysis, <u>calculus</u> **deals with** rates of changes of functions. There **are** <u>two principal areas of calculus</u>: differential calculus and integral calculus. <u>Differential calculus</u> **provides** a way of calculating maxima and minima of functions and instantaneous rates of changes of functions as opposed to an average rate. With integral calculus, <u>we</u> **are able to calculate** areas and volumes bounded by curves and surfaces with precision, to find lengths of curves, and to determine divergence or convergence of an infinite series of numbers.

(Wright 1994: 163)

Subjects and Verbs: Example 2

By means of outer sense, a property of our mind, <u>we</u> **represent** to ourselves objects as outside us, and all without exception in space. In space <u>their shape, magnitude, and relation to one another</u> **are** determined or determinable. <u>Inner sense</u>, by means of which the mind intuits itself or its inner state, **yields** indeed no intuition of the soul itself as an object; but there **is** nevertheless <u>a determinate</u> form [namely, time] in which alone the intuition of inner states is possible, and <u>everything which belongs to inner determinations</u> **is therefore represented** in relations of time.

(Kemp Smith 1933: 67)

FIGURE 7.4 Two examples of paragraphs containing elaborate sentences (The main subject is underlined and the main verb is emboldened for each sentence.)

shows it with Example 2. If you find this all very difficult to follow, you may want to skip Figures 7.4 to 7.6 just now and return to them when you are more confident with the ideas.

In the analysis in Figure 7.5, by separating out the main words in the subject, verb and object we get a clearer picture of what calculus is all about. In missing some words out, I am not denying their importance – they are essential – but I am exposing the structure of the sentence. You might want to try doing this with Example 2 in Figure 7.4 before looking at my version in Figure 7.6.

The main point here is to keep coming back to:

the verb	what is doing, happening or being
the subject	who or what is actively doing the verb or passively having it done
the object	who or what is the receiver of action of the verb.

If you can understand subjects, verbs and objects, then you can write good sentences. Complements, conjunctions, compound and complex sentences all add to this knowledge. So do phrases and clauses – main clauses and dependent clauses. The Glossary at the end of this book defines all of these terms. Don't worry if you haven't understood them all. I had to look some of them up myself to make sure I was using the appropriate expressions!

7.4 The sentence and punctuation

Chapter 9 is devoted to punctuation in sentences; here we are mainly concerned with the notion that a sentence starts with a capital letter and ends in a full stop. This is not strictly accurate. There are three ways of finishing a sentence, the full stop being the most common:

a full stop (sometimes called a *period*)	.
a *question mark*	?
an exclamation mark	!

Barbara likes chocolate.
Does Barbara like chocolate?
Barbara is obsessive about chocolate!

For academic writing, you are mostly likely to use the first. You probably should be answering questions rather than asking them and the exclamation mark suggests a sensational use of language that is inappropriate for academic writing.

If you are using any of these punctuation marks, then you will probably

Subject	Verb	Object
1. ... calculus	deals with	rates of changes...

I am using three dots ... to show that I have omitted something.
'A branch of analysis' is an additional description of calculus. It is really part of the subject.
'of functions' gives more detail about the object; it is really part of the object.

2. two principal areas of calculus	are	differential calculus and integral calculus (not an object – a complement)

There is no object here; the 'there' construction has been used to set up the subject and there is a complement (the two types of calculus). Note that you could reverse the sentence: *Differential calculus and integral calculus are two principal areas of calculus.*

3. Differential calculus	provides	a way of calculating...

The rest of the sentence is also part of the object. Note that the object is compound. It's again referring to rates of changes and to functions

4. ... we	are able to calculate... to find... to determine...	areas and volumes... lengths... divergence or convergence...

'integral calculus' is the topic of this sentence, but is not the subject. 'With integral calculus' is a phrase – an important one saying something about the verb – but the grammatical subject is 'we'.
The 'to' form of the verb, the infinitive, cannot stand on its own but in this case has 'are able' as an auxiliary. This auxiliary does a lot of work here, helping three infinitives, each having an object.
The first and third objects are both compound and there are other ideas to do with curves and series that need to be taken into account.

FIGURE 7.5 Analysis of the sentences in a sample from *Introduction to Engineering*. (Wright 1994) (see also Figure 7.4).

Subject	Verb	Object
1. ... we	**represent...**	**objects**

There is a subject, verb and object in this sentence and each is elaborated quite a bit.
The first phrase is itself elaborated with the second phrase – saying how we do the representation. These are phrases rather than clauses as there is no verb.
'to ourselves' is an important phrase following the verb, again saying how we do the representing.
The words after objects say something about objects (which is itself the object of the sentence).

2. ... their shape, magnitude, and relation to one another	**are**	**determined or determinable** (not an object – a complement)

'In space' is an important phrase saying where this happens – it relates to 'are'.
Because 'are' is from the verb 'to be', I am suggesting that 'determined or determinable' is a compound complement. If it were just the word 'determined' I would have preferred to talk about this as the passive and put the word in with the verb. In either case, there is no object.

3. Inner sense...	**yields...**	**no intuition...**

There is a clause that describes inner sense.
The word 'indeed' is an adverb, emphasizing the verb 'yields'.
'of the soul itself as an object' is an important part of the object.

4. a determinate form	**is**	**time** (not an object – a complement)

Note that this is a compound sentence, joined with 'but' as well as a semicolon.
It is also a complex sentence, where there is a clause that makes a comment about 'time' – 'a determinate form' that is the subject of the sentence.

5. everything...	**is...represented**	(no object)

The full subject of the final main clause is:
everything which belongs to inner determinations

This long sentence needed the semicolon as well as the 'but' as even the second part of the sentence is itself compound, joined with 'and'.
Though there is no object, the phrase 'in relations of time' explains how the representation is done.
The missing expression after 'everything' is a vital part of the subject. The writer is not talking about everything, but about '**everything which belongs to inner determinations**'. Note in particular that there is no comma in this subject. In Chapter 8, I explain why this is important.

FIGURE 7.6 Analysis of the sentences in a sample from Kant's *Critique of Pure Reason* (see also Figure 7.4).

have a main clause including at least a verb and a subject. There are other useful marks in sentences – especially commas – and we deal with this in more detail in the following two chapters. If you find you are using a lot of words in a sentence, to the extent that it is becoming hard to read, you may need to think about punctuation to help you – including using the full stop a bit more frequently. However, at this stage, there is one other punctuation mark to think about with respect to sentences; this is

a semicolon   ;

This is a particularly useful mark as it can be used in the same way as a conjunction in compound sentences. That is, it can act instead of 'and' to link two sentences of equal weight.

Barbara likes chocolate; she prefers it to beer.

We can put the semicolon to immediate use to solve a typical student problem: running sentences together.

7.5 How to avoid running sentences together

A recurring problem with student essays is that sentences run together. Very often, a student puts in a comma, because 'it sounds like a short pause'. When you have two main clauses a comma is not (usually) strong enough to separate them. I can always think of exceptions in elegant writing, but the use of the comma to 'splice' two sentences is generally unacceptable and considered a particular fault in student writing. (You may remember it was number 10 in lecturers' pet hates in Chapter 1.)

There are several reasons why a comma splice happens. I have identified some typical ones in Figure 7.7. I've provided a possible correction. Below, I have summarized the approaches I have taken in this figure to avoid using a comma splice.

Some alternatives to comma splices are:

1 Rewrite the sentences to reduce the number of main clauses.
2 Substitute the subject of a clause with a linking word (typically change 'this' to 'which') and keep it as one sentence.
3 Use a semicolon before words such as 'however' or 'therefore' that introduce new main clauses.
4 Put in another full stop to separate the sentences.
5 Turn one of the sentences into a dependent clause.

Reason	Typical 'wrong' sentence using a comma splice	Possible correction
1 The writer is unaware that there are two main clauses.	This essay is about cause and effect, it argues that the relationship does not have to be mechanical.	This essay argues that the cause and effect relationship does not have to be a mechanical one.
2 The writer does not realize that 'This' is a subject rather than a linking word.	It is important first to look at the way we use language, this affects how we understand the nature of causes.	It is important first to look at the way we use language, which affects how we understand the nature of causes.
3 The writer thinks that 'however' should be used as a conjunction to join two main clauses. (It should not.)	If one event occurs immediately after another there may be a causal connection, however, there may be no necessary connection between them at all.	If one event occurs immediately after another there may be a causal connection; however, there may be no necessary connection between them at all.
4 The writer has got so carried away with the message that the sentence has not stopped.	We have discovered that there is a difference between sufficient and necessary conditions, there is also a difference between causally necessary and logically necessary conditions.	We have discovered that there is a difference between sufficient and necessary conditions. There is also a difference between causally necessary and logically necessary conditions.
5 The writer has not identified a subordinate relationship for one of the two clauses.	We may need to retain the idea of the Causal Principle, science as we know it could not operate without it.	We may need to retain the idea of the Causal Principle, because science as we know it could not operate without it.

FIGURE 7.7 Comma splices and how to avoid them.

Although the comma splice is one of the most common ways of running sentences together, it should be noted that run-on sentences can happen without commas too! This is why it is so useful to understand about finite verbs and their subjects. If you have two finite verbs and two subjects, you need some devices to avoid running them together. These devices might have different functions for the sentences:

Coordinate	with a word like 'and', 'but', 'so' or a semicolon
Subordinate	with a word like 'when', 'because', 'although'
Separate	with a full stop

Subordinate clauses are another name for dependent clauses and we'll be looking at them in more detail in Chapter 8. If you subordinate a clause then you make it lower in rank – that is, you don't allow it to be a main clause, but it says something about the main clause.

7.6 How to avoid chopping sentences in two

The other main problem with sentences comes when they are not complete. They are not sentences at all, even if they follow the rule 'Start with a capital letter and end with a full stop.'

Number 5 of the lecturers' pet hates in Chapter 1 was when students write sentences without verbs. This would clearly be one of the causes of an incomplete sentence. It is not the only one, however. We have already seen that as well as a verb, a sentence needs a subject. So if a sentence is missing a verb or a subject, then it is likely to be incomplete. The result is sometimes called a 'sentence *fragment*' (Figure 7.8); if you get a message from a grammar checker that you have one of these, then check your subjects and verbs. Again, there are a number of reasons for a sentence fragment.

Some alternatives to sentence fragments, then, are:

- Use a *colon* to separate the main clause from an explanation.
- Bring the fragment back into the previous sentence. Use a comma to separate a subordinate (dependent) clause from a main clause.
- If the fragment is long, or hard to relate to the previous sentence, put in a subject and a finite verb.
- Make sure that any commentary has a subject and a finite verb.

So it's not so much that people don't finish their sentences; it's more often the case that they put the ending into a new sentence. The incomplete bit often follows on from a complete sentence. In fact, it ought to be a subordinate clause.

Reason	Typical sentence fragments (underlined)	Possible correction
1 The writer thinks a full stop is needed as there would be a significant pause in speech.	There was a significant event that influenced Galileo's thinking about how the universe works. <u>The invention of the telescope</u>.	There was a significant event that influenced Galileo's thinking about how the universe works: the invention of the telescope.
2 The writer does not realize that 'which' is a linking word rather than a subject.	Galileo noticed that four small 'stars' near Jupiter were in fact revolving around the planet. <u>Which contradicted astrology and religion</u>.	Galileo noticed that four small 'stars' near Jupiter were in fact revolving around the planet, which contradicted astrology and religion.
3 The writer thinks that a present participle is sufficient action in the sentence; however, a present participle is an incomplete verb.	Copernicus had earlier suggested that the earth moved round the sun. <u>Convincing Galileo at an early age</u>, though he kept quiet about it at first.	Copernicus had earlier suggested that the earth moved round the sun. This had convinced Galileo at an early age, though he kept quiet about it at first.
4 The writer wants to make a brief observation, without explicitly stating an opinion.	Galileo realized that the teachings of Aristotle and the Church were inaccurate. <u>A dangerous view</u>.	Galileo realized that the teachings of Aristotle and the Church were inaccurate. This proved to be a dangerous view.

FIGURE 7.8 Sentence fragments and how to avoid them.

Again, what is really important is to make sure that you have a main clause with a subject and verb and to create appropriate links or separation from other clauses.

7.7 Sentences and paragraphs

Lecturers hate it when you . . .

* make every sentence a paragraph;
* don't use paragraphs.

(Pet hates number 6 and 7, from Chapter 1.)

Sentences provide the building blocks for paragraphs, another bugbear for Kim and a source of annoyance for lecturers. It seems that some students make every sentence a paragraph and others don't have any paragraphs at all. Both stem from the same cause; writers don't know what a paragraph is for.

Paragraphs should be visible, either because there are spaces between them or they are indented from the margin. The former is now more common, though many textbooks (including this one) still use indentations to indicate new paragraphs. Spacing uses up more paper. If you are not indenting, then you should consider using extra spacing even if your essay is already double-spaced because a paragraph does need to be clearly separated from the next one. You may lose marks unnecessarily if a lecturer can't see where your paragraphs are supposed to end.

I particularly welcome Gowers's (1973) view (see Bibliography), shared by other writers, that paragraphs provide breaks for the reader. This takes away from the idea of 'what's right' and emphasizes 'what helps', which seems a good principle to follow. The eye gets a rest after a suitable input of information. So a paragraph represents a chunk of information around an idea. If there is a shift in direction, then a new paragraph is necessary. If there seems to be too much to take in, then it is a good idea to look at an appropriate place for a break.

Very short paragraphs suggest a short attention span. You will see them in tabloid newspapers and in children's books, for example. In academic writing, you are more likely to be expanding on a particular point, so if you have a short paragraph you possibly have not said enough about that point. Ask yourself whether you need more evidence, more examples, more details or an alternative perspective.

Often, a paragraph expands on a main statement, sometimes known as a *topic sentence*. This is quite likely to be the first sentence in the paragraph; sometimes it is the last one. The rest of the paragraph gives additional detail around this main point, either expanding from it or building up to it. This is a very useful thing to know; if you have to read a book very quickly, it may be possible to get the gist from reading the first sentence of each paragraph. For example, here is the first sentence (or part of it) from each of the first seven paragraphs of Chapter 17 of Bill Bryson's book: *A Short History of Nearly Everything.*

1 Thank goodness for the atmosphere.
2 The most striking thing about our atmosphere is that there isn't very much of it.
3 For scientific convenience, the atmosphere is divided into four unequal layers; troposphere, stratosphere, mesosphere and ionosphere . . .
4 Beyond the troposphere is the stratosphere.
5 After you have left the troposphere the temperature soon warms up again . . .
6 Even so, spaceships have to take care in the outer atmosphere . . .
7 But you needn't venture to the edge of the atmosphere to be reminded of what hopelessly ground-hugging beings we are.

In general, each of these first sentences is followed by some useful detail. The third paragraph concentrates on the troposphere, which is the first subtheme mentioned in the first sentence, and in this case the most important one. Notice how at the start of paragraphs 4 to 7 there are words that show the change of direction: beyond, after, even so, but. So there is a change of direction with a change of paragraph but it is 'signposted'.

Bill Bryson is an excellent writer, though occasionally his language is slightly more informal than the academic texts you will probably be reading and writing yourself. If we look at his first paragraph, we can see how it expands from the initial topic sentence:

> Thank goodness for the atmosphere. It keeps us warm. Without it, Earth would be a lifeless ball of ice with an average temperature of minus 50 degrees Celsius. In addition, the atmosphere absorbs or deflects incoming swarms of cosmic rays, charged particles, ultraviolet rays and the like. Altogether, the gaseous padding of the atmosphere is equivalent to a 4.5-metre thickness of protective concrete, and without it these invisible visitors from space would slice through us like tiny daggers. Even raindrops would pound us senseless if it weren't for the atmosphere's slowing drag.
>
> (Bryson 2003: 313)

There are six sentences in this paragraph.

1 The topic sentence – an expression of gratitude for the atmosphere. This also an interesting example of a subjectless sentence, though there is an implied 'we'.
2 The first reason for being glad of the atmosphere (warmth).
3 Explanation of the first reason.
4 The second reason (protection).

5 Further elaboration of how we're protected.
6 Further elaboration including implications of not having the atmosphere.

Block	Made up of...
Verb	Person, and tense. Possibly participle and auxiliary verb.
Sentence	Verb and subject. Possibly object, complement, adverb, adjective, phrase or clause, conjunction and other linking words.
Paragraph	Topic sentence(s). Possibly other sentences providing detail, evidence, explanation, elaboration, development of the topic.

FIGURE 7.9 Building blocks: verbs, sentences, paragraphs (see also FIGURE (ii) at the start of the book).

So the whole paragraph expands on why we should be pleased about the atmosphere: it keeps us warm and protects us. This then sets the scene for the next paragraphs, looking at how the atmosphere is formed and how each layer affects us.

Once you become familiar with how paragraphs build up and link together, you'll be able to do it yourself. Don't be afraid just to write things and then organize it into an appropriate sequence and clear paragraphs later.

In the dialogue at the beginning of this chapter, Abel was right to say that we're looking at building blocks. Verbs are at the heart of these and they themselves may be built up.

This seems like a lot to think about, but we put these things together all the time in day-to-day speaking and writing. The analysis is given here to show how it works, not to provide a formula for every sentence you write, as that would take for ever. As always, you are encouraged just to keep writing and then worry about what it looks like through a reader's eyes later. But don't forget this final stage.

7.8 Sentenced to death!

Barbara, Abel and Kim have been through a few grammar books and put together some observations about sentences, a bit like the ones above. They'd like to write a reply to the journalist who said that students can't write in sentences, but after all their efforts, they don't know where to start.

Barbara: If you look at what the lecturers have marked in red, most of the time our sentences are fine. Just occasionally, we run them together or chop them up. I chop 'em up – but I know why. It's the way I speak and hear it in my head. I think it's just a matter of checking.

Kim: I run everything together – sentences, paragraphs etc. – so I can get it all down. Then I throw in a few commas. But I will start looking for subjects and verbs; it's not that difficult.

Abel: I probably haven't been pulled up for it so much because I used to copy the sentence structure from the books I was using! But I was nearly in trouble for plagiarism, which is much worse.

Kim: But it's useful to think of that. You can copy sentence structure without plagiarizing, as long as you're not using the same ideas. So copy the shape of the sentence, but have a different subject, different verb.

Barbara: Yes, I need to use more signpost words like 'although' and 'however'. I'm going to look for other examples – see how the books do it.

Abel: Signposts – you mean, words that point to where the argument's going. I like that idea. I'm going to try that too. *[See Figure 8.2 for some examples of signposting.]*

Kim: So – we sometimes make mistakes, 'cause we don't check enough or we haven't been aware of some things. Doesn't mean we *can't* write sentences – we write loads of them. But I've had enough of sentences – I'm sick of 'em. I've just got one more for you; I'd like you to come to my party.

She hands Barbara a card.

Abel: Don't I get an invite?

Kim: One per couple. These cost a fortune to print. And it's the last time I'm saying or writing the word 'sentence' today.

You have been found guilty of being considered OK by Kim.
Your sentence will be to attend:

A Rocky Horror
Birthday Party

**20 May from midnight
(after the showing of the
Rocky Horror Picture Show)**

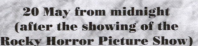

Bring a ghoul if you want.

7.9 Comments on questions

1 How would you define (a) a sentence and (b) a paragraph?

(a) This is a difficult question. My own preference is to say that a sentence is a group of words forming a grammatical unit, including at least a verb and a subject. However, I am able to find exceptions to that definition. Other definitions suggest that the group of words should include the expression of a topic, and begin with a capital letter and end with a full stop. Some people define sentences in terms of clauses: a clause is a subject and something that is said about it (also known as a *predicate*) and a sentence is a group of words with at least one main clause.

(b) A paragraph is a collection of sentences forming a unit. Paragraph breaks give readers a rest and allow them to see that a change in direction is signposted.

2 What are the main things that go wrong with sentences – either your own or other people's?

There are two main things that go wrong: sentences are run together or they are cut in half.

Another criticism of sentences is that they can become too convoluted; they are perhaps grammatically correct, strictly speaking, but they become very difficult to follow. You may need to think about how you punctuate very long sentences. In the next two chapters, we shall look more closely at punctuation of sentences – particularly in Chapter 9.

7.10 Conclusion: advice about sentences

Students can – and do – write in sentences all the time. A few errors keep recurring. The following points may help you to avoid these common mistakes.

- Get used to the structure of subject, verb, object.
- Use conjunctions to make your sentences more elaborate.
- A comma followed by 'this', or 'however' may be a sign of a comma splice.
- A sentence that starts with 'which' may be a fragment.
- A verb ending -ing is not complete and needs an auxiliary to be in a main clause.
- Paragraphs should give readers a break.
- There is often a topic sentence at the start of a paragraph.

7.10.1 Technical terms relating to this chapter

For further information, look up these words or phrases in the Glossary, other grammar books or the World Wide Web.

Adverbial clause
Clause
Comma splice
Compound sentence
Conjunction
Coordinating conjunction
Dependent clause
Ellipsis
Fragment
Intransitive verbs
Object
Predicate
Run-on sentence
Subordinate clause (another word for dependent clause, see Chapter 8)
Subordinating conjunction
Topic sentence
Transitive verbs

8

Relationships and relatives

8.1 Oh brother! • 8.2 Questions about relationships and clauses •
8.3 Words expressing relationship • 8.4 Revisiting the subordinates •
8.5 Relative clauses – defining and describing a brother • 8.6 Every
which way but that • 8.7 Comments on questions • 8.8 Conclusion:
advice about relative clauses

- *Are you commenting on the action, subject or anything else?*
- *Are you defining or describing something else in the sentence?*
- *Which words are your signposts?*

In this chapter, we look more closely at how to expand a simple sentence using dependent clauses. In Chapter 7, we saw how conjunctions could be used to create clauses that were dependent or subordinate to the main clause. There are other kinds of subordinate clauses too, with different types of link. In particular, students often have problems with what are called 'relative' clauses – and our case study shows some problems with other kinds of relatives as well (brothers!).

Relative clauses act like adjectives; they say something about a noun in the sentence. In the story, they say something about brothers, but it could easily be something else – such as photosynthesis or postmodernist thought!

8.1 Oh brother!

Kim has a lot on her plate just now. She has a reason for wanting to sort out her sentence structure that she has not yet explained to Barbara and Abel and she's beginning to feel uncomfortable about keeping secrets from them. This is particularly difficult as Barbara is staying in her flat for a while, because her own has developed some unpleasant leaks.

It's just as well that Kim is in a large flat and that her two flatmates have disappeared on a three-month placement. Kim comes from a big family and two of her four brothers have decided they want to stay with her for a few days before her party. She has masses of coursework to do, especially as she is in her final year. Her dissertation and her presentation are particularly worrying her. She's finding herself distracted by some of the grammar issues and she's also seen a competition she wants to enter with a laptop for a prize, because she needs a new one. The competition involves writing a romantic short story – it's not her sort of thing, but she thinks she'll give it a go.

And, of course, she has a party to organize. She doesn't really know anything about *The Rocky Horror Picture Show*, but it had seemed like a good idea at the time when she heard that the film was coming to town. The discussion about tenses (Chapter 4) had got her singing the 'time warp' song, so she blames that.

Today Kim has a meeting with her tutor at 4.30 pm, she's supposed to be going to a football game at 6.00 pm with Barbara and Abel, and her brother Derek from Dundee has announced that he'll be arriving in time to go to the football too. She might not get back to the flat in time to meet Barbara and Abel. She leaves a note for Barbara:

I've gone to see my tutor. My brother, who comes from Dundee, will be coming with us to the football. I'll meet you there.

Barbara is multitasking: she is eating chocolate, doing some reading for her project, and thinking about why Kim gave her and Abel a joint invitation as a couple. The door bell goes at about 5.15 pm. When she answers the door, there is Abel and a guy that looks a bit like Barbara's type (though she admits herself that that covers quite a wide range).

Abel:	This is Kim's brother – just met him outside. He's come to stay.
Barbara:	Oh, that's great. She did leave me a note. You have to come to the football with us. What's your name? I'm Barbara.
Eddie:	I'm Eddie. I think I'll just wait here if that's OK. I've got some papers to read. I'm a vet student – got a dissertation due in.

Barbara: No, no she said you had to come. I've got to take you. I think we'd better go now in fact. The road's busy and there aren't many buses. I'm ready – just dump your bag and we'll get going.

Barbara bustles Abel and Eddie out and they get to the football match in good time. Kim is waiting for them at their usual place and she's got another man with her, who also looks like he might be Barbara's 'type'.

Kim: Hi Eddie – goodness, Barbara how did you persuade him to come? He hates football. This is Derek, my brother who comes from Dundee. I met him off the train.

Barbara: I thought Eddie was your brother!

Kim: He is. Eddie is my brother who lives in Edinburgh. You're probably going to meet Harry tonight as well. Harry's my brother who's still from around here – like me, he didn't move very far from home. And my other brother, Jack, who is coming to the party too, is building a house in Newcastle. So soon he'll be my brother who comes from Newcastle.

Barbara: But your note said your brother would be coming with us.

Kim: My brother who comes from Dundee.

Eddie: And your brother who likes football. I'm your brother who doesn't and who has a dissertation to write. I'm your brother who got hijacked by your bossy flatmate.

Barbara: I think there was something wrong with your note. It would have been easier if you had given his name. Then your brother Eddie, who is obviously too clever to go to football games, could have stayed at home.

Abel: Can someone tell me what is going on?

Eddie: It's her relative clauses. Kim never knows whether she's defining or describing her relatives.

8.2 Questions about relationships and clauses

1 Here is a set of *relative pronouns*. Can you put the correct one in the sentences that follow? (There may be more than one possible correct answer.)

   who, whoever, *whom, whose*, which, what, that

This is the house . . . Jack built.
Abel did . . . he could to finish his essay.

The brother . . . comes from Dundee is Barbara's favourite.
The brother . . . bag is still in the flat wants to go back now.
Kim's favourite person, . . . pays for Eddie's ticket, will be rewarded with a beer.
Kim can't be too hard on Barbara from . . . she has borrowed £10.
Kim is having a party, . . . will happen next weekend.

2 What is the difference between the following two pairs of sentences? How do the commas change the meaning?

My brother, who comes from Dundee, will be coming with us.
My brother who comes from Dundee will be coming with us.

Your brother, who is too clever for football, is going home.
Your brother who is too clever for football is going home.

8.3 Words expressing relationship

If you are a native English speaker, you probably did not have too much difficulty with Question 1 above, though there were a couple of possible traps. I wondered about bothering you with the information that these words are called 'relative pronouns', but I have decided that it is useful because the label might draw attention to what is going on here.

Question: Why is it useful to know about relative pronouns?
Answer: If you use them properly, you may avoid chopping sentences up.

These little words can often result in problems in students' writing. We saw in Chapter 7 that the relative pronoun 'which' is sometimes used mistakenly as the subject of a sentence. Another kind of pronoun, 'this', should be used instead. The following sentences illustrate the different uses.

I have a birthday party to go to, which will cost me a lot of money.
I have a birthday party to go to. This will cost me a lot of money.

If you want more information on different types of pronoun, see Appendix 1. It shows, for example, that some of the words we are using here can also be used as pronouns to start questions. A lot of words in English can be used in more than one way and this does cause some confusion.

In the examples in Figure 8.1, however, we are thinking about the words as relative pronouns – words that introduce a certain type of clause – and there are a few things that can be said about using them correctly. A pronoun is used as a substitute for a noun; when it is relative, it *relates* to another noun or pronoun in the sentence.

To see if you can understand this, can you find the noun that each example in Figure 8.1 relates to?

	Meaning, example and notes
who	This means 'the person or people which'. It is used of people, where 'which' is used of things. **The people who are entering the competition have a week to write their story.**
whoever	This is more general: it refers to 'everyone who' or 'whatever person'. It is similar in use to whatever, wherever etc. Sometimes, 'ever' is used after 'who' in other ways, and this causes some confusion. **1. The winner of each section, whoever writes the best story of its genre, will receive a laptop.** 2. Who ever saw such beautiful people? (In the second example, 'who' is a different kind of pronoun – interrogative – and does not belong here. See Appendix 1.)
whom	People often worry about whether they should use 'whom'. It is used when 'who' becomes the object of the sentence. **She is the person whom I contacted about the competition.** Nowadays, the word is often not used when it might sound stilted. Above, it could be omitted or replaced with 'that'.
whose	This is a *possessive* for both 'who' and 'which' – in other words, it doesn't just need to apply to people. **The company whose competition Kim is entering lays great stress on good writing.**
which	'Which' is the relative pronoun used of things rather than people. **Kim is entering the competition, which closes a week on Friday.**
that	'That' can be used to replace 'who' 'whom' or 'which', especially if it is defining something. Grammar checkers on computers often suggest 'that' instead of 'which' especially if there is no comma before it. It is not necessary to make this substitution, though some people prefer it. **Barbara wants to know about the competition that Kim is entering.**
what	Although 'what' can be used as a relative pronoun, it should not be used to replace 'which' (though this is quite common in some dialects). It can be used for 'that which' or 'those which', for example: **Kim is studying for what she hopes is her last exam.**

FIGURE 8.1 Relative pronouns.

The nouns for each relative pronoun are:

who = people
whoever = winner
whom = person
whose = company
which = competition
that = competition
what = exam

8.4 Revisiting the subordinates

Before we look in more detail at how we can use these relative pronouns, I want to come back to the idea of clauses. This section reviews what I have said about them already, and extends the notion of subordinate or dependent clauses.

Chapter 7 considered three types of sentence: simple, compound and complex. These are summarized below.

1 Simple: What's the action and who or what is the subject of it?

There is one main clause, with a subject and verb. It possibly includes adverbs, adjectives and other nouns (e.g. object or complement). The example below has a subject, verb, object and adverb.

Abel plays tennis regularly.

2 Compound: What actions and subjects have equal importance and can be joined together?

There are two or more simple sentences joined with a conjunction. 'But' is a conjunction that links or coordinates two sentences where one has a contrasting meaning to the other.

Abel plays tennis regularly but he has gone to the football game today.

3 Complex: What can we say about the action, subject or object?

A comment is made on the main clause, with a subordinate or dependent clause. 'Although' is a conjunction that indicates that there is something to say about the main clause, in this case admitting that something is different to what might be expected.

Abel plays tennis regularly, although he has gone to the football game today.

We saw that conjunctions could act as 'signposts' to show the answers to the questions like how, where, why and when. Now we can add two more questions – what and who – and use relative pronouns to introduce other subordinate clauses.

Abel plays tennis, which he prefers to football.
Abel, who plays tennis regularly, is fitter than Derek.

These clauses act like adjectives – that is, they describe a noun (Abel in the examples above).
    'What' can also be used to create clauses that work like nouns.

Abel believed what Kim had told him about Barbara's feelings.

In this case, the clause acts as the object of the sentence.
    Subordinate clauses, then, can act in the same way as:

adverbs   saying how, why, when and where something happened
adjectives   saying something about a noun or pronoun in the sentence
nouns   being a subject, object or other noun or pronoun

(See Appendix 2 for more details on this.)
    Remember, a clause always has a verb in it and that verb will usually have a subject. A subordinate clause expands the main clause in some way. It is also known as a dependent clause, showing that it depends on the main clause.

I am not a grammarian. To me a subordinate clause will for ever be (since I heard the actor Martin Jarvis describe it thus) one of Santa's little helpers.
                                                                 Truss (2003: 32)

Question: So why bother about subordinate clauses?
Answer: Knowing about subordinate clauses can help you to 'signpost' your writing better. It is also useful to know what they are so you can get rid of them if you have too many.

Now that we have added 'who' and 'what' to the way we can expand our main clauses, it is perhaps worth bringing together some of these linking words as a set of potentially useful expressions for essays and reports. Some of the examples in Figure 8.2 can also be used for phrases rather than clauses – and, in fact, too many clauses can cause problems.
    You can often replace subordinate clauses with simpler expressions, without

To show...	Example link words	Some subordinate clauses
when	after, before, until, when, while	while the investigation was happening
where	where, wherever	wherever the incidents have occurred
why	as, because, since	because there is insufficient evidence
what	which, that	which will be a method for testing the hypothesis
who	who, whose, that	whose research has made a significant contribution
what conditions are necessary	if, unless	if the tests prove positive
concession	although, even if	although many writers agree
comparison	as if, like	as if the opposite had been the case

FIGURE 8.2 Subordinating and signposting.

verbs. If your sentences are getting complicated, with too many subordinate clauses, think about simplifying the clauses into phrases.

- while the investigation was happening – during the investigation
- because there is insufficient evidence – because of insufficient evidence
- . . ., which will be a method for testing the hypothesis – . . ., a method for testing the hypothesis

So I'm not necessarily encouraging you to use a lot of subordinate clauses. They can be the cause of the 'convoluted' sentences that were lecturers' 8th pet hate in Chapter 1; they may also be related to number 9 about pompous language. And I've already pointed out that knowledge about clauses can help you avoid number 5 (sentences without verbs) and 10 (run-on sentences).

But subordinate clauses do have their uses. The next section considers two of these: defining and describing.

8.5 Relative clauses – defining and describing a brother

In this chapter, I am particularly interested in relative clauses. This is not just because Kim has so many relatives: it is also because the confusion at the football match showed two different types of relative clauses. I hope you realize that you don't have to be talking about brothers to use relative clauses; however, Kim's brothers do bring out the distinction between these two types. As Eddie pointed out, Kim needs to be sure whether she is defining or describing her brother (Figure 8.3).

Note that if you were speaking the two sentences in the examples, the intonation would be slightly different in each.

In the case of defining, the meaning might have been clearer if it had been used in a contrast between the two brothers.

My brother who comes from Dundee will go to the game, but my brother who comes from Edinburgh hates football.

Again, it should be noted that the whole situation would be much simpler and clearer without unnecessary verbs:

My brother from Dundee will go to the game, but my brother from Edinburgh hates football.

Sometimes, however, we do need a relative clause that defines or restricts a noun or pronoun. In Chapter 7, in Figures 7.4 and 7.6, we saw the expression from Kant's *Critique of Pure Reason*:

everything which belongs to inner determinations

	Example	Notes
Describing	My brother, who comes from Dundee, will go to the game.	In this case, the expression 'who comes from Dundee' is an additional part of the sentence. It is not essential to the meaning, but is an aside. We can tell this because commas have been used to enclose the expression. (In Chapter 9, we look in more detail at the use of commas for enclosing.)
Defining	My brother who comes from Dundee will go to the game.	Here, the expression 'who comes from Dundee' has not been separated off as a description. It defines which brother is being talked about.

FIGURE 8.3 Relative clauses that describe or define.

There I made it clear that the 'which belongs to inner determinations' was a necessary part of the subject of the sentence. The clause is not a description of 'everything'; it is a definition of what is covered by 'everything'.

This is a tricky distinction and Chapter 9 returns to it, to emphasize the importance of punctuation. But our students have found another problem with relative clauses that define and describe: should they be using 'which' or 'that'? I should point out that I wouldn't be mentioning this at all myself if grammar checkers didn't make such a fuss about it!

8.6 Every which way but that

Back at the flat. Eddie has decided to forgive Barbara for dragging him to the football, but only because he wants to borrow her dictionary and get her to help proofread his dissertation. Barbara is rather grumpy because she thought he had been rude to her because of a simple misunderstanding over commas. She'd also rather talk to Derek than think any more about grammar. You may notice this in her responses.

Eddie: Can you just read this sentence; there's something funny about it.

Barbara: Well it doesn't make me laugh. It just sounds wrong. Why are you saying 'that' here? 'The author, that spent his placement in Fife, acknowledges the support of three local veterinary practices.' 'That' refers to things, not people, surely. Well, of course you may have a point . . .

Eddie: No, I've been told that 'that' can refer to people too. Especially in *restrictive clauses.*

Barbara: In what?

Eddie: Restrictive clauses. I don't know what that means though. Can you look it up in your dictionary?

Barbara: [Sighs] OK. Restrictive. *[Reads from The Chambers Dictionary, 2003]* It says here: 'expressing restriction, as in relative clauses, phrases etc. that limit the application of the verb to the subject. Look, it gives an example – very appropriate: '*People who like historic buildings should visit Edinburgh.*'

Eddie: Oh, so it's like, defining.

Barbara: Yes, people who like historic buildings – and no commas. And yes, you probably could say 'people that like historic buildings . . .'. It's like in the definition: 'phrases that limit the application' – there you could say 'which' instead of that.

Eddie: Ah, then I'm not right because it's not restrictive. It's descriptive: it should be 'The author, who spent his placement in Fife . . .' It's just that the grammar checker keeps telling me to replace 'which' with 'that'. And I knew you could replace 'who' with 'that' sometimes too.

Barbara: *[Annoyed]* You're making my head spin. And it sounds suspiciously like the same point you were making about brothers from Dundee and Edinburgh. Are you sure you know what you're talking about?

They go and borrow a couple of Kim's grammar books and put together the following information. Barbara added the examples: she said she was fed up with types of clauses having so many different names and it's easier to remember examples. (I tend to agree with her!)

Use...	Example
which for things in descriptive or *non-restrictive* clauses	This book, which I have found helpful, is due back at the library.
who for people in descriptive or non-restrictive clauses	The lecturer, who had a PhD, knew the answer to my problem.
which OR **that** for things in defining or restrictive clauses	The book which is overdue must be returned immediately; you can keep the other one.
	OR
(use **that** if you want to keep the grammar checker quiet!)	The book that is overdue must be returned immediately; you can keep the other one.
who OR **that** for people in defining or restrictive clauses	The lecturer who had a PhD knew less than the other one.
	OR
	The lecturer that had a PhD knew less than the other one.

FIGURE 8.4 Which or that?

Eddie: So grammar checkers aren't always right.
Barbara: And neither are you.

It is important to let you know about this. I have heard of cases where lecturers, perhaps influenced by grammar checkers, insist on 'that' instead of 'which' in cases where the clause is defining the subject. Current grammar books suggest the attitude is old fashioned; it is probably a case where the language is in the middle of a change. It is as well to know that people have different views on this. The problem with the grammar checker is that it is not always able to tell what your context is. There will be more on this problem in Chapter 11.

8.7 Comments on questions

1 Here is a set of relative pronouns. Can you put the correct one in the sentences that follow? (There may be more than one possible correct answer.)

who, whoever, whom, whose, which, what, that

This is the house **that** (or **which**) Jack built.
Abel did **what** he could to finish his essay.
The brother **who (or that)** comes from Dundee is Barbara's favourite.
The brother **whose** bag is still in the flat wants to go back now.
Kim's favourite person, **whoever** pays for Eddie's ticket, will be rewarded with a beer.
Kim can't be too hard on Barbara from **whom** she has borrowed £10.
Kim is having a party, **which** will happen next weekend.

In the last example, 'that will happen next weekend' doesn't actually sound wrong and I suspect that some writers (for example, Palmer, 2003) would be quite happy with it.

2 What is the difference between the following two pairs of sentences? How do the commas change the meaning?

My brother, who comes from Dundee, will be coming with us.
My brother who comes from Dundee will be coming with us.

Your brother, who is too clever for football, is going home.
Your brother who is too clever for football is going home.

In each case, the first example describes the brother and is not an essential part of the subject of the sentence. In the second example the clause is used to specify which brother is being referred to.

This chapter has spent some time on the distinction between describing and defining, which Chapter 9 will revisit.

8.8 Conclusion: advice about relative clauses

- Use 'who' (or 'whom', 'whoever' or 'whose' as appropriate) for people and 'which' for things.
- You can replace 'who' or 'which' with 'that' in restrictive clauses, though you don't have to.
- Think about whether you want your clause to describe (non-restrictive) or define (restrictive); you don't need to remember these names, but you do need to know where to put the commas.

8.8.1 Technical terms relating to this chapter

For further information, look up these words in the Glossary, other grammar books or the World Wide Web.

Adverbial clause
Non-restrictive clause
Noun clause
Phrase
Possessive
Relative clause
Relative pronoun
Restrictive clause
Subordinate clause

9

How to be offensive with punctuation

9.1 Define without commas • 9.2 Questions about punctuation • 9.3 The functions of punctuation marks • 9.4 Putting punctuation to work • 9.5 Abel's dodgy colon and Barbara's full stop • 9.6 Comments on questions • 9.7 Conclusion: advice about punctuation

- *Does your punctuation show the reader how groups of words should be read?*
- *Does your punctuation complete, introduce, separate, enclose, or omit?*

9.1 Define without commas

Kim and Barbara are having some toast in the flat before going to university and the mail arrives. Kim's brother Eddie, who went back to Edinburgh to hand in his dissertation, has sent her a letter. He has a special message for Barbara, but Barbara doesn't get to that bit as when Kim shows her the letter she is so incensed about the third sentence.

Kim: Pompous git. Who writes letters these days? Why not just send me an email? Do you want to see it?

Barbara: No, I like getting letters. I think it should be encouraged; it's more personal. But yeah, let's see it.

> **Extract from Eddie's letter**
>
> Dear Kim
>
> Thanks for letting me stay last week; I really appreciated it. I even started to enjoy the football, though the fans spoiled it a lot. English football fans, who get drunk and fight at matches, should be ashamed of themselves. It doesn't happen in Scotland of course!
>
> It was good to meet your "grammar pals" and I particularly look forward to seeing Barbara again on Saturday. I have a little surprise for her, to thank her for her help with my dissertation.

Kim: Here you are – there's a bit about you in it anyway. He seems to have taken a shine to you – it's not like him! I'd better tell him you're spoken for.

Barbara: What do you mean? I'm not spoken for. *[She starts to read]* Oh that's ridiculous. Look what he's saying about English football fans. I'm English. I really object to that, Kim!

Kim: I just skimmed over that bit. Yes, I see what you mean. That's pure racist. Especially when we know he knows what he's saying. He knows about relative clauses – we talked about it.

Barbara: Who'd have thought that two little commas could be so offensive?

Kim: It does make me think that punctuation matters. I didn't used to think that it did.

9.2 Questions about punctuation

1 Do you think the sentence in Eddie's letter is more offensive with or without commas? Why?

2 This question relates to the joke behind the title of Lynne Truss's book (*Eats, Shoots & Leaves* – see Bibliography).

What are the main differences between the two pandas:

(a) The panda eats shoots and leaves.
(b) The panda eats, shoots and leaves.

3 If you look for other punctuation jokes on the internet, the main one you find is a version of the following. A professor asked a class of students to punctuate this sentence.

Woman without her man is nothing

(a) How did the boys punctuate it?

(b) How did the girls punctuate it?

4 Punctuate the following sentences so that any ambiguity – which may even be offensive – is removed. In most cases, you'll have to put in punctuation but you may need to take some out as well.

(a) Abel laughed and joked about failure an hour after Barbara failed her exam

(b) What a mess you have made a difference already though

(c) I've got a friend who could ask for anything more

(d) When Kim plays the saxophone sounds out of tune

(e) I'll give Kim, a bag, a box of chocolates and a birthday card

(f) Kims birthday presents are the following a DVD of the *Rocky Horror Show* the theme for her party cakes, iced with her teams colours to improve her punctuation; a book and a comic recording *Phonetically Speaking* by Victor Borge a bedroom scene a painting she likes chocolates and a bag to hide other unwanted presents

(g) Isnt that touching Barbara said Abel have you seen the bloke you used to go out with his friend is Kims brother Welsh friends are here too it seems we've got plenty of men if youre looking for someone new Im not the one I want already knows who she is dont you

9.3 The functions of punctuation marks

The main function of punctuation is to support meaning. It shows us how a group of words should be read together. It lets us know where to stop and what to keep separate. It may tell us that a group of words is an aside: for example, a description or a comment. It may even tell us that there is something missing. If you have any doubts about the value of punctuation, here is a well-written paragraph with the punctuation removed, along with the capital letters that indicate a new sentence. You might want to consider where the punctuation marks should go. (The untampered version is in Section 9, after the answers to the questions.)

There are I suppose only a few works that seem even more essential to the Western Canon than *Paradise Lost* Shakespeares major tragedies Chaucers *Canterbury Tales* Dantes *Divine Comedy* the Torah the Gospels Cervantes *Don Quixote* Homers epics except perhaps for Dantes poem none of these is as embattled as Miltons dark work Shakespeare undoubtedly received provocation from rival playwrights while Chaucer charmingly cited fictive authorities and concealed his authentic obligations to Dante and Boccaccio the Hebrew Bible and the Greek New Testament were revised into their present forms by redactionists who may have shared very little with the original authors whom they were editing Cervantes with unsurpassed mirth parodied unto death his chivalric forerunners while we do not have the texts of Homers precursors

(Bloom 1994: 26)

Many people (not everyone), seeing such a passage, would try to work out which words go with which. Sometimes it is quite easy to do this; sometimes you need a little help. This is what punctuation is for: to help you to work out which words go together and how they would sound if they were said out loud.

For some people, the words go together like music – they hear a set of words in their heads as they might hear a set of notes that naturally go together. We use the same word for this process, with both words and music: phrasing. When Kim realizes this, the penny drops. She has been practising the saxophone to play at her party and suddenly she is aware that she is thinking about punctuation as she is playing the piece.

Kim: 'Let's do. The time-warp. A-gain.'

Well, it might punctuate the music but it makes a bit of a mess of the sentence if you're saying it normally. But yes – it is almost the same thing. The musical notation tells you where to stop, where to pause, what bits go together, where the emphasis goes. That's all it is. I need to turn my sentences into music!

Kim realizes that she's talking to herself and goes off to find Barbara and Abel. Barbara is still staying with her and Kim thinks Abel might be there too, but he's out playing tennis. Barbara is at the kitchen table dreamily moving around 'Post-it' notes. She has written words on each and is trying them out in different sequences. Kim reads some of these.

| since the start of the twenty first century | because it is important to find out the cause of the problem | which is the main reason for the success |

Kim: You've got hundreds of these. What on earth are you doing?

Barbara: I've been going through some books looking for useful expressions for essays. There are loads of them; I've been using them already whenever I'm stuck for something to say.

Kim: They seem to be bits of sentences: phrases and clauses.

Barbara: Yes – they're words that go together, but they still need to be put with main clauses. It's like Abel was saying about building blocks. I haven't really thought about words working together before.

Kim: I was just thinking about that with music too . . .

Barbara: I heard you!

Kim: . . . and I think it might help with punctuation. You know, sometimes you have to stop. Sometimes you need to separate out bits that go together, like phrases. Sometimes you're almost saying 'here's a little aside'. There are signs in music to help you with these things; I suppose punctuation's a bit like that too.

Barbara: I don't know what you're talking about. I don't read music or anything like that. But I can see the same thing with these Post-its. Some of these are words I want to keep together. And then I might need to make it clear that they belong to each other and are separate from another bit of the sentence.

The doorbell rings, and Abel is standing there flushed after his game of tennis, but he starts talking almost as soon as Kim opens the door.

Abel: It was hard to concentrate on the game, 'cause I kept thinking about punctuation! Each rally was like a sentence and the lines of the court turned into commas or full stops. If you were outside the line, you had to stop and start again. It was like a new sentence!

Barbara: I think you've both gone mad. Punctuation is about words, not tennis movements or musical notes!

Kim: Well, we each have our own ways of thinking about things. And it doesn't hurt anyone. But we're all talking about stopping things, separating them . . .

Barbara: Making little asides

Kim: . . . and interrupting what I'm saying. I think Abel and I are thinking about rhythms, and you're more interested in the way things look.

Abel: Different learning preferences. You need to think about that if you're a teacher. So some kids would be more likely to remember things they hear and some things they see. Or even do. So you have to vary the way you teach them.

Barbara: Is there any point to this?

> Kim: Yes – lots of points. Punctuation points. I've just never thought about what they're for. Let's put them together and see what we come up with.

Using some of the language books they've been looking at, the students try to identify the different functions of different punctuation marks. The result is in Figure 9.1.

Figure 9.1 shows punctuation in its role within sentences. It looks at marks by function: completing, separating, enclosing and omitting. These are the main things that you have to do in sentences.

There are some other punctuation marks too, which do things within individual words rather than sentences. They are used for abbreviations (full stop and apostrophe), joining (*hyphen*) and omitting (apostrophe). We'll be looking at these in Chapter 10 and particularly the apostrophe. You may remember from Chapter 1 that the misuse of the apostrophe is lecturers' number 1 pet hate. Because of this, I decided that it should have a chapter (almost) to itself.

9.4 Putting punctuation to work

As well as being necessary for understanding, punctuation is used by skilful authors to create an effect. Here is a passage from an old edition of Charles Dickens's *Pickwick Papers*, where an eccentric character called Mr Jingle, a rascal, has a very distinctive way of speaking. The punctuation helps us to 'hear' his voice, which gives us more information about his personality. The long dash usually indicates omissions or interruptions. Dickens has stretched this convention to convey Jingle's jerky and incomplete speech.

> 'Ah! You should keep dogs – fine animals – sagacious creatures – dog of my own once – pointer – surprising instinct – out shooting one day – entering inclosure – whistled – dog stopped – whistled again – Ponto – no go; stock still – called him – Ponto, Ponto – wouldn't move – dog transfixed – staring at a board – looked up, saw an inscription – "Gamekeeper has orders to shoot all dogs found in this inclosure" – wouldn't pass it – wonderful dog – valuable dog that – very.'
>
> (Dickens 1837/1963)

While you wouldn't write an academic work in such a way, it is useful to see how punctuation contributes to the meaning. Notice as well that the whole passage is in single inverted commas, but Jingle wants to quote something himself so that statement has to go into double inverted commas. (It doesn't matter which way round you do this as long as you are consistent.)

Completing
You must have one of the following at the end of each sentence.

Mark	Name	Function	Example
.	Full stop or period	Marks the end of a sentence.	The two writers interpret the same information in very different ways.
?	Question mark	Marks the end of a question.	What methods are available for analysing such data?
!	Exclamation mark	Ends a sarcastic or emphatic statement. (Best to avoid.)	Readers can make what they want of that statement!

Introducing
Use one of these to introduce a distinctive part of the sentence

Mark	Name	Function	Example
,	Comma	Introduces direct speech.	One student reported, 'I think I have done enough to pass.'
:	Colon	(a) Introduces a list, after a word that sums it up.	Lecturers have several complaints: poor punctuation, poor sentence structure, inadequate paragraphing, and wrong use of words.
		(b) Introduces a quotation or direct speech (as an alternative to a comma).	Mark Twain said: 'When angry, count a hundred; when very angry, swear.'
		(c) Introduces an explanation or particular example.	There is another punctuation mark that you should know: the apostrophe.
–	Dash	Indicates a change of direction, or significant follow up.	This view of the world was accepted for centuries – then Newton made his important discovery.

(continued)

Separating
Use one of these to separate parts of a sentence.

Mark	Name	Function	Example
,	Comma	(a) Separates a phrase or dependent clause, especially if it comes first.	Because the essay was late, the student got a reduced mark.
		(b) Separates items in a list.	The main consequences of failure of this equipment are accidents, delays, loss of material, and financial penalties.
		(c) Separates direct speech from the speaker. Note that the comma is before the quotation mark.	'I think I have done enough to pass,' she said.
;	Semicolon	(a) Separates items (e.g. in a list) that already contain commas, or are quite long.	The study considered three main areas of research: the effects of frequent use of drugs; the roles of the mother, father and siblings in the behaviour of the young person; the impact of custodial sentences on reoffending.
		(b) Acts as a conjunction.	The third theory was tested first; it was thought the easiest.

(*continued*)

Enclosing

To enclose information in a sentence, use one of these pairs.

Mark	Name	Function	Example
, ,	Commas	Separate an aside or extra phrase that the sentence does not need grammatically.	The result, which was a surprise, was a win for our team.
( )	Parentheses	(a) Indicate an aside that is interesting but not very important.	We discovered (as did previous researchers) that consistency was crucial to the study.
		(b) Used in some forms of citation to provide information given in more detail in the references.	According to Chandler (1995), academic writers adopt various different strategies.
[ ]	Square brackets	(a) Often used to insert editorial/explanatory comments on another's writing.	The student claimed: 'We benefited most when our TMA [tutor marked assignment] was returned to us within a week.'
		(b) Can be used in numerical referencing systems.	The findings by the first researchers [16] were quite unexpected.
– –	Dashes	Separate with more emphasis than commas.	The third group – all mature students – demonstrated the most unusual approach to the project.
' ' " "	Quotation marks/ *inverted commas*	(a) Enclose direct speech. Use single or double, but be consistent.	McLuhan said, 'The medium is the message.'
		(b) Highlight the first use of an unfamiliar word or phrase	This type of drawing is usually known as a 'free body diagram'.
		(c) Indicate the title of a chapter or journal article	Bartholomae, D. (1985). 'Inventing the university' in M. Rose (ed.), *When a Writer Can't Write*. New York and London: Guilford Press.
	Scare quotes	(d) Draw attention to a word or phrase. Don't overuse.	This 'prediction' turned out to be false.

(*continued*)

Omitting

To show that something is missing, use the appropriate one of these.

Mark	Name	Function	Example
...	Ellipsis	Trailing off a thought. Missing word(s). Useful for quotes. The example uses what the writer thinks is important, but shows there were other words.	Smith (1999) said: 'Students... will use a range of intelligences.'
——	Long dash (Printers would call it a two em dash)	A name or other word is omitted.	A study was undertaken at —— University to find out about students' grammar.

FIGURE 9.1 Functions of punctuation marks in sentences.

9.5 Abel's dodgy colon and Barbara's full stop

Time is getting very tight for Kim. She's making notes for her talk to the industrial sponsors, hearing the rhythms of her own speech in her head as she writes. It's flowing quite well. Barbara and Abel are sitting together in the next room proofreading her dissertation: Kim hopes that this will bring them closer together. Unfortunately, her romantic notions about them are not helped by the fact that Abel is feeling unwell and Barbara is just irritable. However, their conversation contains some useful observations about punctuation.

Abel: I've had an idea for the title. What do you think, Barbara? 'Vibrations, colon, minimizing and avoiding them.'

Barbara: We're proofreading, Abel, not editing. Leave her title alone – there's nothing wrong with it. Why do you want a colon anyway?

Abel: I've noticed a lot of colons in titles. People seem to use a colon to introduce a sort of subheading. *[He pulls a journal from his bag.]* Here's one from the *British Journal for the Philosophy of Science*. 'Structure: its shadow and substance'. So it's like an announcement, then an explanation. It seems appropriate for what Kim's trying to do.

> *Barbara:* That's a style thing. We're just looking for anything that's obviously wrong. Like commas. She's still putting them in the wrong place and it interrupts the flow of the sentence. Listen: 'Vibrations in machines, platforms and other structures [pause] cause extra stress and energy loss.' She doesn't need a comma after 'structures' – why has she put one in?
>
> *Abel:* I agree with you. It doesn't make sense to separate the subject and the verb with a comma.
>
> *Barbara:* Mmm. Useful rule. *[She writes it down.]* She's probably done it because it's a compound subject and it does make sense to have a comma after 'machines'. But that's all she needs.
>
> *Abel:* Here's a colon I want to take out. 'A position of stable equilibrium, colon, restoring forces will return the system to this position.' I think she's trying to give an explanation after the colon, but it needs to be introduced by a complete sentence.
>
> *Barbara:* Let's see? Yes, I think she should just say: 'Restoring forces will return the system to a position of stable equilibrium.' Either that or 'A position of stable equilibrium is required, colon, restoring forces etc.' It's making my head spin.
>
> *Abel:* So what's the rule? If you're using a colon as a sort of introduction to an explanation, then there has to be a complete sentence before it.
>
> *Barbara:* Yeah – I'll write that down too. You seem to be obsessed with colons today, Abel.
>
> *Abel:* Well, my own's not feeling too good. Barbara, I'm going to have to quit. I'd a greasy meal late last night. I'll have to leave you to it, I'm afraid.
>
> Abel returns home, much to Barbara's annoyance as they have all sorts of arrangements for Kim's party to finalize. She continues with her proofreading and decides that the list of rules she has started is a useful one, so she keeps going. When Kim triumphantly finishes writing her speech at 1.30 am, she comes into the kitchen and finds Barbara fast asleep, slumped over the dissertation, with a list of suggestions and a separate list of rules ('don'ts') for punctuation by her side.

9.5.1 Some useful 'don'ts' for punctuation

These are based on the most common errors that students make. (Kim seems to be a typical student!)

- Don't separate a subject and verb with a comma.
- Don't use a comma to separate complete sentences.

- Don't use a comma unless it helps the reader's understanding.
- Don't use a colon to introduce an explanation unless there is a main clause before it.
- Don't use a colon to introduce a list that completes the sentence (e.g. We are learning grammar, language and punctuation.).
- Don't use a semicolon to introduce a list; use a colon instead.
- Don't use quotation marks too often to replace 'so-called': both read like sneering!

If all this seems like a lot to remember, then don't try to. Don't let worrying about punctuation slow your writing down; you can always correct it later. If you know that you have a tendency to make a mistake in one particular area – such as using commas instead of full stops – then do a special proofread looking just for this.

Apart from apostrophes, commas are the most frequently misused punctuation marks. They are likely to have too much work to do, be in the wrong place, or be missing when they are needed for sense.

Many students avoid colons and semicolons altogether because they do not know how to use them. Some famous writers have also avoided them for a variety of reasons (see Truss 2003 for some examples). I agree with Truss that these punctuation marks are graceful, helping authors to write with style. And often punctuation is just a matter of personal style. If you're scared to use colons and semicolons, then they can be avoided by careful writing. But it is still worth knowing what their functions are.

9.6 Comments on questions

1 Do you think the sentence in Eddie's letter is more offensive with or without commas? Why?

This is the same point that was made in the last chapter about whether a clause defines or describes a noun. In Eddie's version, he is making a statement that describes English fans. This assumes that all English fans get drunk and fight. If you remove the commas, then he is specifying which fans should be ashamed of themselves.

2 This question relates to the joke behind the title of Lynne Truss's book:

What are the main differences between the two pandas:

(a) The panda eats shoots and leaves.

(b) The panda eats, shoots and leaves.

The first panda behaves very typically and the compound object of the sentence is 'shoots and leaves'.
   The second panda does three things; this is a compound sentence with three verbs. (One subject covers them all.)
   The comma changes the intonation of the sentence as well as the meaning.

3 If you look for other punctuation jokes on the World Wide Web, the main one you find is a version of the following. A professor asked a class of students to punctuate this sentence.

   Woman without her man is nothing

(a) How did the boys punctuate it?
     Woman – without her man – is nothing.
(b) How did the girls punctuate it?
     Woman – without her, man is nothing.

(There are various alternative possibilities.)

4 Punctuate the following sentences so that any ambiguity – which may even be offensive – is removed. In most cases, you'll have to put in punctuation but you may need to take some out as well.

(a) Abel laughed and joked about failure an hour after Barbara failed her exam
     Abel laughed and joked about failure. An hour after, Barbara failed her exam.
     This makes the timing of his laughing clearer. Knowing Abel, he probably still felt bad about it though!
(b) What a mess you have made a difference already though
     What a mess! You have made a difference already though.
     So we know it's not you that made the mess!
(c) I've got a friend who could ask for anything more
     I've got a friend. Who could ask for anything more?
     Not a greedy friend who keeps asking for things!
(d) When Kim plays the saxophone sounds out of tune
     When Kim plays, the saxophone sounds out of tune.
     The saxophone needs tuning. It's not that Kim's a bad player.
(e) I'll give Kim, a bag, a box of chocolates and a birthday card
     I'll give Kim a bag, a box of chocolates and a birthday card.
     Kim might not like being described as a bag!
(f) Kims birthday presents are the following a DVD of the *Rocky Horror Show* the theme for her party cakes, iced with her teams colours to improve her

punctuation; a book and a comic recording *Phonetically Speaking* by Victor Borge a bedroom scene a painting she likes chocolates and a bag to hide other unwanted presents

Kim's birthday presents are the following: a DVD of the *Rocky Horror Show* – the theme for her party; cakes, iced with her team's colours; to improve her punctuation, a book and a comic recording (*Phonetically Speaking* by Victor Borge); a bedroom scene (a painting she likes); chocolates; and a bag to hide other, unwanted, presents.

If you're making comments within a list, it's important to know what goes together. Kim wants these presents so the commas round 'unwanted' make a huge difference here.

(g) Isnt that touching Barbara said Abel have you seen the bloke you used to go out with his friend is Kims brother Welsh friends are here too it seems we've got plenty of men if youre looking for someone new Im not the one I want already knows who she is dont you

'Isn't that touching, Barbara?' said Abel. 'Have you seen the bloke you used to go out with? His friend is Kim's brother. Welsh friends are here too. It seems we've got plenty of men, if you're looking for someone new. I'm not. The one I want already knows who she is . . . don't you?'

There are various ways you might punctuate this. You need to know whether Barbara or Abel is the one who is talking. This could also tell you whether Abel is gay or not. I have put an ellipsis (. . .) before the last question to suggest that there is something unspoken here. It is possible to use punctuation to create an impression, though you probably won't do this much in academic writing.

This is the punctuated version of the paragraph in Section 9.3.

There are, I suppose, only a few works that seem even more essential to the Western Canon than *Paradise Lost* – Shakespeare's major tragedies, Chaucer's *Canterbury Tales*, Dante's *Divine Comedy*, the Torah, the Gospels, Cervantes' *Don Quixote*, Homer's epics. Except perhaps for Dante's poem, none of these is as embattled as Milton's dark work. Shakespeare undoubtedly received provocation from rival playwrights, while Chaucer charmingly cited fictive authorities and concealed his authentic obligations to Dante and Boccaccio. The Hebrew Bible and the Greek New Testament were revised into their present forms by redactionists who may have shared very little with the original authors whom they were editing. Cervantes, with unsurpassed mirth, parodied unto death his chivalric forerunners, while we do not have the texts of Homer's precursors.

(Bloom 1994: 26)

9.7 Conclusion: advice about punctuation

If you're getting confused over punctuation, it may be that you are still sorting out the ideas that you want to write about. It's a good idea to get your ideas down and then worry about the punctuation later. Here are some tips to help you when you are reading over your own work:

- Use punctuation to help you to complete sentences and alert readers to appropriate groupings of words within them.
- Think about whether you are completing, introducing, separating, enclosing or omitting.
- Read your work aloud to help you to hear the rhythms of your sentences.
- Ask someone else to proofread your work and tell you when they are puzzled about something you have written. It may be that the punctuation is not helping the meaning.
- Make a special check for punctuation that you know you often get wrong.

9.7.1 Technical terms relating to this chapter

For further information, look up these words in the Glossary, other grammar books or the World Wide Web.

Bracket
Colon
Comma
Dash
Ellipsis
Full stop
Inverted comma
Parenthesis
Period
Question mark
Quotation mark
Scare quotes
Semicolon

10

Possessive apostrophes and missing letters

10.1 Kim gets possessive and goes missing again • 10.2 Questions about punctuation in individual words • 10.3 Hyphens and stops • 10.4 What's happening to the apostrophe? • 10.5 How to use an apostrophe while you still can • 10.6 Hold the apostrophe! • 10.7 That Lynne Truss has a lot to answer for! • 10.8 Comments on questions • 10.9 Conclusion: advice about apostrophes and other marks

- *Do you need punctuation to join, abbreviate or omit letters in words?*
- *What use is the apostrophe?*

Chapter 9 concentrated on punctuation of sentences. This chapter considers punctuation of individual words and just three punctuation marks: the hyphen (-), the period (.) and the apostrophe ('). The most mistakes – by far – happen with the apostrophe, so most of the chapter is about this. We have reached number 1 in lecturers' pet hates.

10.1 Kim gets possessive and goes missing again

Barbara has left Kim a note on the kitchen table.

I have finished proof-reading and have left you a list of mistakes and rules. I also counted up the numbers for your party: you have fifty odd friends coming. Your brother's pal rang and asked you to phone him back. Abel's auntie, Mrs. O'Brien, rang too. Abel isn't well and may miss the party.

Luv Babs

Kim looks at the note and snorts. She doesn't notice Barbara coming back into the kitchen.

Kim: Why are my friends odd? Who puts a full stop after Mrs nowadays? And which brother's pal?

Barbara: Fifty-odd friends. Perhaps you should reduce that by one: you sounded sneery about me there. And I think Calum is a friend of both Eddie and Derek, from the way he was talking, anyway. Posh bloke.

Kim: Oh Barbara – sorry. I didn't see you. I've been waiting for two calls, actually. Calum is Eddie's and Derek's friend but Joe is just Eddie's friend; Derek can't stand him. And I can't stand Calum!

Barbara: Oh, happy families again.

Kim: Actually, if it was Calum who rang, your note should have the apostrophe after the s, because he's the friend of my two brothers.

Barbara: Since when did you become an expert on the apostrophe?

Kim: Since I finished this book. [She shows Barbara **Eats, Shoots & Leaves** by Lynne Truss.]

Barbara: Did Abel give you that for your birthday? We were going to get you that and other stuff together. Wait till I see 'im! I'll kill 'im.

Kim: Don't get 'em in a twist. I'm not bothered who gets what. And you don't need to get me anything – really. No need for a lovers' tiff.

Barbara: I don't know where you get this idea from Kim . . .

Kim: Eddie's got plans for you anyway. I think Calum's his little surprise for you. He's an expert on grammar, but he's always sneering at people who can't afford to go to posh schools like the one he was at. I think Eddie thinks you'll fancy him. Maybe that'll make Abel jealous.

Barbara: Your brother's a pest! Your brother Eddie, anyway.

Kim: Now, now – he's OK. He's got his faults, but haven't we all? I'm the only one allowed to criticize him.

> Barbara: And why should I fancy Calum if he sneers at people?
>
> Kim: You'll need to learn some put-downs for people who sneer. Our grammar's getting pretty good and we've done it all ourselves – we didn't have his advantages. Thanks for the proofreading, by the way – you missed a few things but you did pick up things that I didn't.
>
> Now, go and make up with Abel and take him some grapes. And you'll need to shift some of this furniture if we've got so many people coming. I'll be out for the rest of the day.
>
> Barbara: But . . .
>
> Kim: And Abel didn't give me the book; I got it at Christmas. But something's clicked and I understand it properly now.
>
> But Kim is already disappearing out the door as she says this and Barbara doesn't hear her. Barbara has too much else to think about anyway.

10.2 Questions about punctuation in individual words

1 In the passage above, what comments might you make about punctuation (or lack of it) in the following expressions:

   (a) proof-reading
   (b) fifty odd guests
   (c) Mrs. O'Brien
   (d) Wait till I see 'im.
   (e) a lovers' tiff
   (f) your brother's a pest

2 What are the main uses for:

   (a) a hyphen
   (b) a period (full stop) to indicate abbreviation
   (c) an apostrophe

and how are these uses changing?

10.3 Hyphens and stops

Before looking at the apostrophe, we'll take a brief look at the hyphen and the period/full stop.

The hyphen has several functions, but its main one is to ensure that the reader doesn't get confused (Figure 10.1). There are also some conventions to observe with hyphens. The main one is to connect words that are used together as an adjective. This only happens before a noun, not after it. For example:

Kim has an up-to-date project.   BUT
Kim's project is up to date.

The main change with hyphens is that they are tending to disappear. But they are still necessary in some cases to avoid confusion.

The full stop or period used as an abbreviation is also tending to disappear. It is now quite rare to see it used in expressions such as:

Mr.   abbreviation for Mister
Mrs.   abbreviation for Mistress, pronounced 'Missus'
Dr.   abbreviation for Doctor

We are so familiar with these terms of address that we no longer need to show that there are letters missing. But it is not wrong to do so.

It is still quite common to see full stops in abbreviations such as e.g. or i.e., though even these are increasingly seen without them. These are abbreviations for Latin expressions and students find them quite useful, though they often use them the wrong way round. Make sure you know what they mean:

e.g.   exempli gratia   for example
i.e.   id est   that is

It is probably better to avoid the abbreviations in formal text anyway and just write 'for example' or 'that is' as appropriate. In general, the advice is to avoid abbreviations.

Both the hyphen and the full stop (used for abbreviations), then, are used less than they used to be. As an expression becomes familiar without one, then we tend to miss out the mark. As always, if in doubt it is useful to check a recently published dictionary.

Possible confusion	Example use	Comments
A word is split over two lines of type and the reader needs to know that it continues.	We want it to be read-able for everyone.	'readable' is one word. Someone seeing 'read' and 'able' on two different lines might try to read the sentence differently. A wordprocessor can be set to do this hyphenation for you. It will break a word in an appropriate place, usually at the start of a syllable.
	However, DON'T split expressions like the following…	
	Today you were not-able by your absence	It would be better to avoid such breaks, even with a hyphen.
	There was need for the-rapists.	
Without the hyphen, the word already has a meaning.	re-covering	= covering again (e.g. furniture)
	recovering	= getting or finding again
Without the hyphen, it is not clear which words should go together.	lead-free petrol	petrol without lead
	lead free petrol	Is this petrol that costs nothing?
Without the hyphen, a compound word looks strange, especially if it is a new expression.	e-mail	As expressions become part of the language, they often lose the hyphen. It sometimes becomes a matter of personal preference: e.g. either e-mail or email would be acceptable now.
Without the hyphen, there may be too many of the same letter in a word.	shell-like	The word 'shelllike' would look very odd because of the triple l.

FIGURE 10.1 Using a hyphen to avoid confusion.

10.4 What's happening to the apostrophe?

There are many debates about the apostrophe. As we saw in Chapter 1, its misuse is lecturers' number 1 hate, but nowadays some lecturers don't know how to use it properly either. Some experts think that the apostrophe has had its day and that it would be better to get rid of it altogether. If it doesn't aid understanding, then what is the point of it?

Other writers – including me – would like to see the apostrophe restored to its proper use. It does help to avoid confusion; as the following examples show, the apostrophe is sometimes actually necessary to know what is happening.

> The authors' work has contributed to government policy.
> The bands' music made T in the Park a success.

Here we know – because of the position of the apostrophe – that more than one author or band was involved. If this is not acknowledged, then perhaps only the last mentioned author or band gets the credit and the others get offended.

A possible problem with the apostrophe is that its uses create other associations.

- It is associated with possession – belonging to something. However, this doesn't apply to *possessive adjectives* and *possessive pronouns* (see Appendix 1).
  The student's book.   BUT   Your book. It is yours.

- It is used for abbreviating words, but then they can sound like other words (especially certain kinds of adjective).
  You're a star.   BUT   Your star is in its ascendancy.
  They're working.   BUT   Their work is important.
  It's beautiful.   BUT   You are the reason for its beauty.

- There are some tricky examples of usage.
  Women's work   Women is already a plural
  Dickens's novels   Dickens' novels would also be acceptable
  Mind your p's   The apostrophe helps the reader to see what
    and q's   is intended

Many writers are aware that there are some awkward aspects to apostrophes, but don't know what they are. They then just tend to shove one in whenever there is an s or never use them at all.

Use an apostrophe before s when…	
you want to show that a singular noun is possessive (owns something)	Kim's brother the apostrophe's use
Hint: if you see two nouns together and the first one ends in s, ask yourself if there is a possessive relationship. Can you replace it with 'the b of a'?	the brother of Kim the use of the apostrophe
you want to show that an *indefinite pronoun* is possessive (see Glossary)	nobody's child if one's husband is the Duke of Edinburgh the child of nobody the husband of one

you want to show that a plural noun that does not end in s is possessive	children's playground
	the playground of the children
	
	Similarly
	  the men's room
	  the women's rooms
	  people's rights

FIGURE 10.2(a) The apostrophe before the s.

10.5 How to use an apostrophe while you still can

Even though there are many public examples of missing or misused apostrophes, it is still an advantage to know how to use them. Figure 10.2 is a reminder; keep it by your side when you're checking over an essay or report before handing it in.

10.6 Hold the apostrophe!

A famous sneer about apostrophes is the expression 'the *greengrocer's apostrophe*'. This refers to the habit of some shopkeepers to add an apostrophe

---

Use an apostrophe after s when…

---

you want to show that a plural noun is possessive	the brothers' homes the apostrophes' use three weeks' time MPs' votes the homes of the brothers the use of the apostrophes the time of three weeks the votes of MPs
you want to show that a singular noun that ends in s is possessive	for goodness' sake for Jesus' sake Dickens' novels for the sake of goodness for the sake of Jesus the novels of Dickens In these cases, we just use the apostrophe because of the awkward sound in adding an additional s. However, it would not be wrong to do so, and it sometimes is seen, e.g. St James's Park

FIGURE 10.2(b) The apostrophe after the s.

before any s. So outside a greengrocer's, there might be a sign saying: 'Carrot's, apple's, potatoe's.' Such signs were often painted on windows of shops, in the days when there were greengrocers.

It's a sign of the times (or perhaps some of my personal habits) that I became more aware of this with chip shops. I used to work next to a busy shop in the centre of Glasgow that sold a variety of foods at lunchtime and frequently put up adverts, sometimes painted on the windows, to announce this. As well as pie's, chip's, roll's etc., I noticed one day that they promised 'deliciou's snack's'. The signwriter seemed to have a rule that if there is an s at the end of a word, it needs an apostrophe before it.

When I ask students what is wrong with such signs, they can always tell me. But then they make similar mistakes themselves. I have on occasion used the 'chip shop apostrophe' myself – though I usually manage to catch it before anyone sees it. I probably miss it sometimes, though; I have seen it done by

Use an apostrophe between letters when…	
you want to abbreviate part of the verb 'to be' or an auxiliary verb	I'm, you're, he's, Barbara's, it's, we're, they're, I'll, I'd, I've
	Note that 'Barbara's' can be short for 'Barbara is' or 'Barbara has' depending on the context.
	Barbara's a lovely person.
	Barbara's gone to shout at Abel.
	Similarly, 'it's' is always short for 'it is' or 'it has'
	It is recommended that you avoid such abbreviations in academic writing anyway. A useful rule is **never use 'it's' in academic writing.**
you want to abbreviate 'not'	won't, shan't, don't, didn't, wouldn't shouldn't
	Again, you wouldn't see these in academic writing.
you're showing that there is a missing letter or group of letters	The most common example is o'clock (of the clock). It's often used to show how people speak, particularly a dropped h or a dropped g:
	I'll kill 'im.
	Huntin', shootin' and fishin'
	It is sometimes used to show abbreviated dates:
	Christmas '99; November '06. It is not, however, necessary when talking about groups of years.
	Remember the 1960s? '68 was especially exciting.

FIGURE 10.2(c) The apostrophe used to show missing letters.

people who definitely know better but have written an email or a note in a hurry. I think what happens is that people 'hear' an apostrophe before an s in their head as they are writing and the wrong version gets written down. This is why checking your work is so important.

An s at the end of the word, then, is a trigger for people to think 'should there be an apostrophe here or not?' Until you are on top of the uses of the apostrophe as shown in Figure 10.2, you won't want to stop yourself at the end of every word ending in s – you'd never get anything written! But it's something to bear in mind when you're checking your work over. And if you're still in doubt, look at Figure 10.3 which may tell you that you definitely don't need one.

The greengrocer's apostrophe – where a simple plural is turned into a singular possessive – is probably the main cause of distress for the many people who would like punctuation to be used properly. It is so public that it encourages even more wrong use. This upset some people so much that they set up an *Apostrophe Protection Society*. You can see their website at www.apostrophe.fsmet.co.uk.

By the way, you should read Lynne Truss's book if you want to know why we shouldn't sneer at greengrocers.

10.7 That Lynne Truss has a lot to answer for!

Why did the Apostrophe Protection Society not have a militant wing? Could I start one? Where do you get balaclavas?

(Truss 2003: 4)

Do I need an apostrophe? NO	Examples
Are the words ending in s just simple plurals?	The sources consulted were academic books and journals, the public records and the local newspapers.
Is 'its' a possessive rather than an abbreviation for 'it is'?	The company is proud of its achievements.
Is the expression any form of possessive pronoun, rather than an abbreviation?	Your books are overdue.
	If it is a problem, it is theirs.

FIGURE 10.3 No apostrophes please.

Things aren't going too well for our students at the moment. Barbara is annoyed with Abel because she thinks he's given Kim their present in advance. She also doesn't like the sound of Calum, though part of her is interested by the attention she's getting. Her essay marks have improved considerably, though for the first time she has failed a small exam and that's making her wonder if she's managing her time properly. Abel is still feeling queasy, is worried about money and is starting to get confused about whether he really fancies Barbara or not – she's becoming too much of a friend! Kim is overdoing everything. Derek saw her disappearing round the corner with a large cardboard apostrophe on a stick and a pot of white paint.

Barbara and Derek are sharing a beer in Kim's kitchen.

Barbara: So what's your friend Calum like then?

Derek: Hard to describe. He's taking the mickey most of the time, so you shouldn't take any notice of him. He's OK. Make sure you know what a *subjunctive* is, though.

Barbara: Oh, so he's sneery. The grammar pals don't like sneering. At least, I thought we didn't. Kim's getting odd about punctuation. It's as if a light's gone on. A week ago, she didn't know anything about commas and apostrophes and that – now she does.

Derek: I don't think she's sneering – it's much worse than that. She's militant!

Barbara: What do you mean?

Derek: Well, I think she's gone out to 'correct' the posters on that shop round the corner.

Barbara: You're joking. She'll get caught.

Derek: She was always passionate about things. Even as a wee kid. We were always rescuing her from fights and arguments.

Abel arrives, with a copy of *Eats, Shoots & Leaves* and a CD.

Barbara: Abel, what were doing you giving Kim her present in advance? It's made her go doo-lally. We agreed that we'd do something together. You really get on my nerves sometimes.

Abel: What are you talking about? I've got part of her present here. Did you get the chocolates and the bag? Here's the book you said to get. And a CD I found. Victor Borge.

Barbara: Oh, I'm sorry. I thought you must have given her it. Well, she's got the book already anyway. We'll have to get something else.

Abel: Barbara, I can't afford anything else. I'm skint, remember. We've got enough here – if you've got your bits that is. This CD's got a track called 'Phonetic Punctuation' – it's dead funny. But don't ask me to spend any more.

> *Barbara:* Well, there might not be a party anyway. Kim seems to have other plans. She's gone out to attack people with an apostrophe on a stick.
>
> *Derek:* I think we need to go and find her. Come on Barbara.
>
> But when they get to the shop round the corner, it's already too late. Kim is outside the shop, painting out the 'apostrophe s' on the notices about chip's and pie's on the window. She doesn't need her apostrophe on a stick; there are extra apostrophes everywhere. But she's noticed that there's one missing in the nearby Travel Agent's and she plans to move on there later, to stand in front of the sign that says: 'Your journeys end – paradise' holding the apostrophe between journey and s. When the others get to her, it's just in time to hear the shop owner shouting: 'And I've called the police.'

10.8 Comments on questions

1 In the passage above, what comments might you make about punctuation (or lack of it) in the following expressions:

(a) proof-reading
(b) fifty odd guests
(c) Mrs. O'Brien
(d) Wait till I see 'im.
(e) a lovers' tiff
(f) your brother's a pest

(a) 'Proof-reading' shows a hyphen used to join together two words. It is an example of an expression that no longer needs the hyphen, because it has become so familiar. While it would not be wrong to write it this way, it is more likely to be one word: proofreading.
(b) This example is a common one used to show how useful a hyphen can be in indicating which words should be read together.
(c) Kim is right to say that people tend not to put a full stop after Mrs, but it still would not be wrong, just very old fashioned. The apostrophe in O'Brien is a very particular usage – it is not an abbreviation of 'of' in the same way as o'clock. It is from an Irish word and is a patronymic meaning 'descendant of' (like the Scottish 'Mac').
(d) The apostrophe shows that a letter is missing. It is often used by writers who are trying to show how someone might speak.
(e) Though there is only one tiff, it takes two people to have it. The apostrophe comes after the s.

2 What are the main uses for:

(a) a hyphen
(b) a period (full stop) to indicate abbreviation
(c) an apostrophe

and how are these uses changing?

(a) A hyphen can be used to link two separate words in a new compound word, break a long word at the end of a line, avoid confusion, show compound expressions before a noun. Its main function is to avoid confusion and if the meaning of a hyphenated expression is clear without the hyphen, it usually loses it eventually.
(b) A full stop can show that a word has been abbreviated. Again, this is a use that is gradually disappearing, as the abbreviated word becomes part of the language. It is now very rare to see stops after abbreviations with capital letters: B.B.C. would look very odd now. Even the lower case abbreviations such as e.g. and i.e. can sometimes be seen without the stops.
(c) An apostrophe is used to show that letters or numbers are missing. One form of this that has evolved from earlier times is to show possession (the *genitive case*). It is also used to avoid confusion – though in practice it actually generates confusion! Because so few people know how to use it, there are predictions that it will disappear altogether. However, it sometimes seems that the opposite is happening.

10.9 Conclusion: advice about apostrophes and other marks

- Use a hyphen to avoid confusion; if you think an expression doesn't need it, it probably doesn't.
- It's better to avoid abbreviations. Once an expression is very familiar or has become an *acronym*, it is unlikely to contain any stops, so you probably won't use the full stop for abbreviations much.
- However, make sure you understand the difference between e.g. and i.e. as they mean different things.
- Never abbreviate 'it's' in formal writing – write 'it is' instead.
- Apostrophes are not used with possessive adjectives: my, your, her, his, its, our, their.
- Apostrophes are not used with possessives without nouns: mine, yours, hers, his, ours, theirs.
- Apostrophes are not used with simple plurals.

- They are not necessary with groups of years, e.g. 1960s.
- When you use an apostrophe to show ownership, the apostrophe goes after the owner.

The woman's book   owner = the woman
The women's room   owner = the women

10.9.1 Technical terms relating to this chapter

For further information, look up these words in the Glossary, other grammar books or the World Wide Web.

Abbreviation
Acronym
Apostrophe
Apostrophe Protection Society
Full stop
Genitive case
Greengrocer's apostrophe
Hyphen
Indefinite pronoun
Possessive adjective
Possessive pronoun

11

Checking the checker

*11.1 A house of correction • 11.2 Questions about grammar checkers •
11.3 Pitfalls with grammar checkers • 11.4 How to use a grammar
checker knowledgeably • 11.5 What happens next • 11.6 Comments on
questions • 11.7 Conclusion: advice about grammar checkers*

* *Do you understand what the grammar checker is telling you?*

Once we know how to do things, human beings like to automate them so we
don't have to worry about them. Automation helps to extend human abilities
by allowing us to do more. Undoubtedly, this makes life a lot easier. We can
calculate a lot of numbers very quickly with calculators and spreadsheets. We
can check our spelling and grammar using spelling and grammar checkers. But
if we don't understand what the calculator or checker is telling us, then we're
not extending our abilities. We are taking a gamble that the technology will do
our work for us.

The main message of this chapter is that the grammar checker should work
with you rather than for you.

11.1 A house of correction

Unfortunately, Kim has been arrested for defacing property (though she insists
that she was un-defacing it). This is not good news; she is due to give a formal

presentation to industrial sponsors the next day and her party is the day after that.

Her friends and brothers are worried that in her excitement she'll make the situation worse. They decide to write a letter to the police explaining the circumstances and take it down to the station later. This is their first draft, typed by Derek in a bit of a hurry.

Dear Sir or Madam
We are written to request leniency in the case of our sister and friend Kim. The removal of apostrophes which she done today were because of her passion for good punctuation. She as been working very hard on her dissertation for university and has a important presentation to do tomorrow. We can ensure you that we wont be letting her do this anymore. Her behavior will be appropriate from now on.
Yours

Barbara is exasperated as she reads over Derek's shoulder.

Barbara: Derek – that's full of mistakes. They'll think we're a bunch of illiterates!
Abel: Barbara! Sneering!
Derek: What does the checker say? Look – there are two squiggly green lines. That means something's wrong. It doesn't like 'apostrophes which' and it doesn't like 'a important'. Oh yes, that should be 'an'.
Barbara: And there's nothing wrong with 'apostrophes which'.
Abel: But there is something wrong with 'which she done'.
Derek: I'll run the checker properly and see what it says. Look, it wants to put a comma after which. I'll just go OK – change.
Barbara: No – you don't need to . . . Oh, now what is it saying?
Derek: Incomplete thought. Right – it wants a verb. So you grammar experts can tell me what verb it wants. What's a verb anyway?
Barbara: Start again. This is a mess.

They muddle through and it still doesn't look right. But when they run the checker again it says: 'The grammar check is complete'.

Abel: Try it at a higher setting – a formal setting.
Derek: *[Changes the setting]* Now it says the first sentence is passive.
Barbara: And I'm not. Or I won't be for much longer.

11.2 Questions about grammar checkers

1 Here is the students' letter again. Can you find all the mistakes? If you can
be bothered, you might like to type it out and run it through your own
grammar checker to see whether it agrees with you.

> Dear Sir or Madam
>   We are written to request leniency in the case of our sister and friend
> Kim. The removal of apostrophes which she done today were because
> of her passion for good punctuation. She as been working very hard
> on her dissertation for university and has a important presentation to
> do tomorrow. We can ensure you that we wont be letting her do this
> anymore. Her behavior will be appropriate from now on.

2 Look back over the topics in this book (for example, look at the contents
page). Which do you think would give the grammar checker the most
difficulty?

11.3 Pitfalls with grammar checkers

Grammar checkers are getting more sophisticated but they still can't tell
exactly what you're trying to say. Many students trust them because they are
so unsure of their own grammar; they assume that the checker must be right.
I often hear students say, 'The grammar checker put a comma there.' But
unfortunately, lecturers will hold you rather than the grammar checker
responsible for wrong spelling and grammar.
    There are various possible pitfalls:

- The checker does not recognize that something is correct.
- The checker does not recognize that something is incorrect.
- The setting is inappropriate; a common example is using a US dictionary for
  work in the UK, resulting in spellings such as 'flavor' instead of 'flavour'.
- The checker can't distinguish between some frequently confused words.
- You can't understand what the checker is telling you.
- If there are a lot of errors, the grammar checker has difficulty in recognizing
  some of them until others are corrected.
- Once you have pressed 'Change' or 'Ignore' then the checker will accept it,
  even if you run it again.
- It is possible to 'teach' the checker to approve of your mistakes – for
  example, by putting a misspelling into its dictionary.
- If you deliberately want to write something that is technically wrong, then

you have to be careful that the checker doesn't change it. This is a problem for writing a book like this, for example. If I want to say that students frequently tell me they are having problems with their 'grammer', I don't want the checker to change this wrong use or my point will be missed!

Figure 11.1 shows another example of a passage that shows some of the pitfalls. It is an exercise that I sometimes use with students as a demonstration of how checkers can be both useful and not useful at once. In Figure 11.2, I show what my own grammar checker made of each sentence.

Your friend has asked you to proofread an essay. Identify spelling mistakes and grammar errors in the paragraphs below, and then compare it with the advice from the grammar checker. NB: there are some mistakes on this page that the Word grammar checker has not picked up.

Studying language

Students must learn to write in the language of there subject area, this is because they are 'trying on' the discourse of that subject. But how are they expected to do this if they have never encountered any writing in this style before. Coming from school or college which means that they have more or less been told what to write. At University it is very different, you have to do your own work and be comitted to finding things out for oneself. If you have wrote something in the wrong style, the lecturers will give you feedback but some writers say that the style should be taught along with the subject mater. Even more than that, errors in grammar occurs because of the complexity of the ideas and not because the student always gets it wrong . Nightingale (1988) suggests that trying to improve grammar without taking context into account is a waste of time. Context is described by some writers as more than just background; it is also an integral part of the practice.

Students are joining new community's of practice and have to learn how they operate. It is wrong from lecturers' to say that there grammar should of been corrected at school, it is up to the lecturers to help them in this new context.

Reference

Nightingale, P. (1988) Language and learning: a bibliographical essay, in G. Taylor, B. Ballard, V. Beasley, H. Bock, J. Clanchy and P. Nightingale (eds), *Literacy by Degrees.* Milton Keynes: SRHE and the Open University Press.

FIGURE 11.1 Do you agree with the grammar checker?

Sentence	What one grammar checker found (and missed)
Students must learn to write in the language of there subject area, this is because they are 'trying on' the discourse of that subject.	It picked up the wrong spelling of 'their' but missed the run-on sentence.
But how are they expected to do this if they have never encountered any writing in this style before.	It didn't like me starting a sentence with 'But' and suggested 'However', which would probably be better for formal writing. If I didn't accept this change, then it missed that this was a question.
Coming from school or college which means that they have more or less been told what to write.	It suggested using a comma after 'college' (correct) or change 'which' to 'that' – so I had to make a choice. It did recognize that this was an incomplete sentence and didn't like the passive.
At University it is very different, you have to do your own work and be comitted to finding things out for oneself.	It picked up the misspelling (committed) but missed the fact that this was a run-on sentence. It wanted a comma after University. It missed the mis-relationship between 'you' and 'oneself'.
If you have wrote something in the wrong style, the lecturers will give you feedback but some writers say that the style should be taught along with the subject mater.	It didn't like the passive construction, but missed the wrong past participle (wrote) and misspelling of 'matter'. ('Mater' is an actual word.)
Even more than that, errors in grammar occurs because of the complexity of the ideas and not because the student always gets it wrong.	It spotted the extra space before the full stop. (This can be very useful.) It missed the mix of singular and plural in 'errors…occurs'.
Nightingale (1988) suggests that trying to improve grammar without taking context into account is a waste of time.	It suggested 'taking context into account' was too wordy and should be replaced by 'considering context' (good idea).
Context is described by some writers as more than just background; it is also an integral part of the practice.	It didn't like the passive and offered a better suggestion: Some writers describe context.
Students are joining new community's of practice and have to learn how they operate.	It suggested, correctly, replacing 'community's' with 'communities'.
It is wrong from lecturers' to say that there grammar should of been corrected at school, it is up to the lecturers to help them in this new context.	It picked up the wrong use of 'of' instead of 'have'. It missed the wrong *preposition* in 'It is wrong from'. It missed the unnecessary apostrophe. It only picked up the wrong 'there' if I corrected the run-on sentence as it suggested, by using a semicolon.

FIGURE 11.2 What the checker finds and misses.

11.4 How to use a grammar checker knowledgeably

Barbara decides to have another shot at writing a letter to the police. She doesn't want to hurt Derek's feelings, but thinks that his effort is unlikely to impress them. As they are using excellence in punctuation as their plea, the letter has to be correct. Here is her attempt.

Dear Sir or Madam

Earlier today Kim W– was arrested for defacing property at a shop on the corner of Argyle Street.

We are a group of students who have been learning about grammar and Kim had been upset about the misues of the apostrophe in the shop. She was editing, she wanted to make the display easier to understand.

Kim has been overworking lately and has a great deal on her mind, including a presentation that she has to make tomorrow (Friday). We wish to make a plea for her release and promise to ensure that she does not cause any further distress.

Yours faithfully

The grammar checker puts a green squiggle under 'was arrested' and a red one under 'misues'.

Barbara: Was arrested – passive. That's OK. I don't particularly want to draw attention to who arrested her! And misues – typing error. I'll correct that. Is there anything else? What about 'who have been learning'? It hasn't marked that. No, it's OK – no commas needed. It's let the comma after 'editing' go, but I think that should really be a semicolon because there are two complete sentences here.

That is the kind of conversation you should have with yourself when you use the grammar checker.

Figure 11.2 shows how a checker can be very helpful, offering useful suggestions for improvement. It also shows that it can miss things or offer inappropriate alternatives because it is unaware of your context. It is important to be able to interpret its messages.

11.5 What happens next?

Barbara takes the letter to the police station, while Derek and Abel go to the shop to see if they can reason with the owner. The owner's son is there, discussing the incident with his dad, and laughing about it. He thinks that Kim has made an improvement and that they should also make a little story about it for the local press. It would be good publicity for the shop. When Derek and Abel say why they have come, the father looks a bit fierce but the son is friendly.

Owner's son: I'll do a short press release about this. I'm supposed to do one for an assignment – I'm doing media studies at the uni.

Abel: I'm at the uni too – and so's Kim, the person who was arrested. Er – you wouldn't want to see a fellow student in trouble, would you?

Owner's son: Depends on the student. I'd have some arrested like a shot. And some lecturers.

Derek: Oh no, I think you'd like Kim. She's great fun. And she'll invite you to her party if you help her out. It's a Rocky Horror Show party.

Owner's son: Oh that party – I've heard about that. Wouldn't mind going to it actually.

They all go to the police station where Barbara is at the counter trying to get attention. She is horrified when she sees who is with them.

Barbara: Mark, what you are you doing here?

It turns out that the shop owner's son is the guy, Mark, who went out with Barbara the previous semester (and who has been the cause of a great deal of her moaning about men).
   A little later . . .

Derek: You lot – you just can't escape punctuation!
Barbara: What do you mean?
Derek: Well, the police are going to question Mark.
Barbara: Doh! That's so not funny.

11.6 Comments on questions

1 Here is the students' letter again. Can you find all the mistakes? If you can be bothered, you might like to type it out and run it through your own grammar checker to see whether it agrees with you.

Dear Sir or Madam
    We are ~~written~~ writing to request leniency in the case of our sister and friend Kim. The removal of apostrophes which she ~~done~~ did today ~~were~~ was because of her passion for good punctuation. She <u>has</u> been working very hard on her dissertation for university and has an important presentation to do tomorrow. We can ~~ensure~~ assure you that we won't be letting her do this anymore. Her behavio<u>u</u>r will be appropriate from now on.

2 Look back over the topics in this book (for example, look at the contents page). Which do you think would give the grammar checker the most difficulty?

Figure 11.3 offers suggestions for this.

11.7 Conclusion: advice about grammar checkers

There is really only one piece of advice about using a grammar checker:

Make sure that you understand what it is telling you.

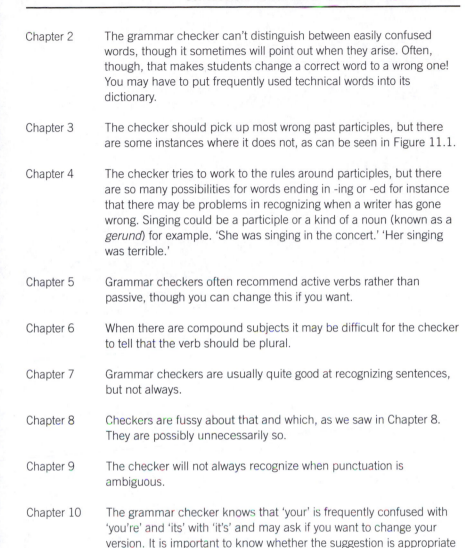

Chapter 2   The grammar checker can't distinguish between easily confused words, though it sometimes will point out when they arise. Often, though, that makes students change a correct word to a wrong one! You may have to put frequently used technical words into its dictionary.

Chapter 3   The checker should pick up most wrong past participles, but there are some instances where it does not, as can be seen in Figure 11.1.

Chapter 4   The checker tries to work to the rules around participles, but there are so many possibilities for words ending in -ing or -ed for instance that there may be problems in recognizing when a writer has gone wrong. Singing could be a participle or a kind of a noun (known as a *gerund*) for example. 'She was singing in the concert.' 'Her singing was terrible.'

Chapter 5   Grammar checkers often recommend active verbs rather than passive, though you can change this if you want.

Chapter 6   When there are compound subjects it may be difficult for the checker to tell that the verb should be plural.

Chapter 7   Grammar checkers are usually quite good at recognizing sentences, but not always.

Chapter 8   Checkers are fussy about that and which, as we saw in Chapter 8. They are possibly unnecessarily so.

Chapter 9   The checker will not always recognize when punctuation is ambiguous.

Chapter 10   The grammar checker knows that 'your' is frequently confused with 'you're' and 'its' with 'it's' and may ask if you want to change your version. It is important to know whether the suggestion is appropriate or not!

FIGURE 11.3 The grammar checker and issues in this book.

12

Finale

Our students are getting ready for Kim's party. For Abel, this means changing his t-shirt. He's not into dressing up, especially in kinky stuff associated with the *Rocky Horror Picture Show*, and he can't afford to anyway.

As Kim dresses up as Frank N. Furter, she reflects on the difference between today and yesterday. Yesterday, she was in a smart suit impressing industrial sponsors with her talk about the role of engineering in environmental improvement. It was very successful; there were no wrong past participles and her passion for the subject shone through her well-prepared talk. She will probably get sponsorship to do a PhD. Today, she will be the centre of attention again – in the role of a mad scientist from the planet Transsexual. She looks at the apostrophe on a stick and decides to take it with her to the film and the party. It will go with the whip. She has promised the police and her friends not to be quite so expressive in correcting people in future, but these are just props.

Barbara has a lot to think about: outrageous costume, make-up, props for the film (she's taking toast, rice, and a newspaper), the bag with Kim's birthday presents. And, most importantly, she has her list of put downs for grammar snobs. She spent half the night with Derek making this up. They can be seen in Figure 12.1.

Unlike the rest of the book, this chapter is more about the soap opera than the points of grammar. Its main function is to tidy up some loose ends. If you want to know more about Barbara's put downs, check them in the Glossary, the internet and other grammar books. The main point about them is that they contain examples of what they are talking about: she's showing she knows the 'correct' version but is trying to suggest that the snob is being unnecessarily fussy.

What Kingsley Amis (see Bibliography) said is the opposite of 'berk' is too rude for this book, so you'll have to look it up somewhere else.

It is surely pedantic to puritanically avoid the *split infinitive*.

If I were you, I'd forget about the *subjunctive*.

Between you and me, I'm not sure that we need to use the *accusative* case after prepositions...

... but if you want *hypercorrection*, then we'll say it's between you and I.

I hope my using a *gerund* doesn't confuse you.

I shall insist on the correct use of '*shall*' or '*will*'. You will help me.

I won't think less of you if you give me fewer *comparative adverbs*.

I think a *preposition* is the best thing to end a sentence up with.

To *whom* am I talking anyway?

Kingsley Amis might describe me as a berk, but we know what he'd say about you!

FIGURE 12.1 Barbara's put-downs for grammar sneering.

After the film, a large number of weirdly dressed students cram into Kim's flat. As Kim plays the saxophone, Barbara finds herself in a line doing the 'time warp' between Calum and Mark.

Calum:	Ah, the grammar girl. The one who won't stand in the queue in Marks and Spencer that says 'five items or less'.
Barbara:	Just give me fewer comparative adverbs.
Calum:	I heard you were pretty hot on the subjunctive too.
Barbara:	Isn't that what Kim's playing just now? If I were you, I'd keep quiet about it.
Calum:	Very good. And where do you stand on the gerund?
Barbara:	I wouldn't want to hurt it. My standing on it would probably kill it.
Mark:	It's supposed to be a party – what's that guy talking about?
Barbara:	Oh well, Kingsley Amis had a word for him. *[She turns to talk to Mark]* Thanks for rescuing Kim, by the way.
Mark:	Sorry I've not been in touch. My dad had a heart attack and I've been looking after the shop. Not easy when you've a load of essays to do. But he's a lot better now, as you saw.
Barbara:	Sorry to hear that. I wondered what had happened.
Mark:	I told him I'd be going out with less girls next semester – just the one, if she'll have me.
Barbara:	Fewer girls. Oh sorry – I didn't mean to . . .
Mark:	OK, let's start again. And this time, no cheating, no standing up – and no sneering.

Barbara: I'm fine with that.

Kim puts down her saxophone and goes over to Abel. He's sitting in a corner looking glum.

Kim: Abel – what are you playing at? Barbara's over there; why aren't you getting together? I might as well let you know, I'm trying to write a romantic story about you – to enter a competition. I need a little crisis, yes, to make the story interesting – but a queasy stomach and being skint is just not going to do it. I want a proper story.

Abel: Well, hasn't she gone off with that rich guy, Calum, anyway? And what story? Haven't you got enough to do?

Kim: I just wanted to try a different kind of writing. A romantic fiction – I had a story about two people falling in love over a participle.

Abel: Oh really!

Kim: It was like a break from engineering – writing I enjoyed doing. And I liked that. Especially when I realized what fun punctuation could be. Thanks for the 'phonetic punctuation' by the way. That was your idea, wasn't it? It didn't seem like a Barbara thing. It's dead funny, but he's kind of right in a way – you can almost hear commas and things sometimes.

Abel: Yeah, I like Victor Borge. But I thought you'd like it because of the way you saw punctuation kind of like music. I'm really getting interested in different ways of teaching people things.

An attractive stranger walks past and hears this.

Sari: You can teach me English. I ask Eddie but he don't tell me things. I'm Sari. Eddie invited me – hope it OK. He say I need practise English.

Abel: Your English sounds very good.

Sari: Can't do *articles* – 'the' and 'a'. Not have in my language. And single and plural not good.

Kim: There we are. You can teach English and grammar, Abel. I'll have to find something else to write about – I'm too late for the competition anyway. And Barbara . . . *[Barbara comes up beside her as she says this]*

Barbara: . . . Barbara what?

Kim: You'll make your mark somehow.

Barbara: Listen. Mark's had a great idea. We've all been writing some of this grammar stuff down and people are getting interested in it. Why don't we write a book and sell it?

Kim: Like, *Grammar without sneering?*

Barbara: Something like that, yeah.
Abel: No, the title's got to have a colon in it. I like colons now.
Barbara: How about *Grammar: A Friendly Approach*?
Kim: It'll never work.

13

Glossary

Don't feel intimidated by this list of words; you don't need to know them all. The definitions are given in case you need an explanation for a word you encounter, for example it might be used in feedback from a lecturer. In the examples, the illustration is of the italicized expression.

Word	Definition and notes	Examples
abbreviation	Shortened word or expression. The example shows the abbreviation i.e. used correctly (see Chapter 10). See also acronym, apostrophe and full stop.	The students had matriculated at the university, *i.e.* they had enrolled with Registry.
accusative case	The form of a noun or pronoun that shows that it is an object. While this is common in many languages, it is rare in English but still exists in words such as 'me' which is the accusative case of 'I'.	She helped *me*. In fact, she helped *Barbara and me*.
acronym	An abbreviation made up of initial letters or parts of words that has now become a word in its own right.	What would we do without *radar*? Most people know that *AIDS* is an acronym; did you know that *amphetamine* is too?
active voice	The form of verb where the subject undertakes the action of the sentence. (Compare passive and see also Chapter 5.)	Abel *questions* his ability to become a teacher.
adjective	A word that describes a noun, pronoun or other adjective.	Kim has very *happy* memories of her party.
adverb	A word that explains how a verb was undertaken (modifies a verb).	Barbara went *happily* to her resit exam.

adverbial clause	A subordinate clause that explains the action of the main clause. See Figure 7.3 for useful conjunctions for introducing adverbial clauses. See also Appendix 1.	He helped me *when I forgot my book*.
agreement	The condition that subjects and verbs match each other in terms of singular and plural. See Section 2.5.	*Abel goes* to the gym; *Kim and Barbara go* to the pub.
apostrophe '	Punctuation mark indicating possession or missing letters. See Chapter 10.	I'll meet *Barbara's* friend at 6 o'clock.
Apostrophe Protection Society	A society dedicated to the proper use of the apostrophe.	The Apostrophe Protection Society's web site can be found at: www.apostrophe.fsmet.co.uk
article	An adjective showing whether a noun is definite or indefinite.	Kim is *an* engineering student. Barbara is *the* student who studies English.
auxiliary verbs	Verbs that are used with participles to help show the tense and mood of the action. See Chapter 4.	I *should have* finished writing my dissertation by the time I go to the party.
bracket [ ]	A punctuation mark, used in pairs, to show that something is enclosed and separated off. See Figure 9.1.	Barbara said, 'He *[Abel]* will be along when he's finished playing tennis.'
clause	A group of words containing a verb (compare phrase). See Appendix 2 for different types of clause.	Abel wants to be a teacher *because he enjoys a challenge*.
colon :	A punctuation mark that introduces something, such as a list, a quote, or an explanation. See Figure 9.1.	Barbara has made a big decision: she is going to major in philosophy.
comma ,	A punctuation mark that separates or encloses. See especially Chapter 9 and Figure 9.1.	Abel said, '*Barbara*, I'd like some help with *commas, semicolons* and full stops.'
comma splice	The error of using a comma to separate two main clauses. See especially Chapter 7, but this is also mentioned as one of lecturers' pet hates in Chapter 1.	There is a comma splice in the following sentence: 'Kim has invited Mark to her *party, this* is because he rescued her.' It would be better to put a semicolon or full stop after 'party'.
complement	A completion for certain types of verb that can't take an object: e.g. to be. See Chapters 6 and 7.	Kim is *a third year student*.
complex sentence	A sentence that has at least one subordinate clause. See Chapter 7.	Barbara is upset *when she sees that Kim has already got the book*.
compound sentence	A sentence that has at least two main clauses. See Chapter 7.	*Barbara is upset* and *she shouts at Abel*.

Word	Definition and notes	Examples
compound subject	The subject of the sentence that has two or more agents. This has implications for agreement. See Chapter 6.	*Philosophy*, which is Barbara's subject, *and the philosophy of science* represent two of the discourses considered in this book.
conjunction	A word that joins two main clauses or a subordinate clause to a main sentence. See Figures 7.2 and 7.3 respectively.	Kim likes music *but* Abel prefers sport. Barbara likes neither, *though* she goes for the company.
coordinating conjunction	A word that joins two main clauses, such as 'and' or 'but'. See Figure 7.2.	The essay is late *but* the lecturer has a lot of marking *and* he won't notice.
count noun	A noun that refers to something that can be counted. It can use words like 'a' and 'fewer'. See Appendix 1.	We can talk about a *song* and fewer *songs*, but we have to say some music and less music.
dangling participle	A participle that is not related to its auxiliary verb or subject. See Chapter 3. This is more formally known as a misrelated participle.	*Drinking* in the last chance saloon. This doesn't make sense unless someone is doing the drinking, e.g. Abel is drinking in the last chance saloon.
dash –	A punctuation mark that is used to introduce a change or significant point, or, in pairs, to enclose. See Figure 9.1.	Barbara – *our youngest student* – learned more grammar at school than the others.
	There are various lengths of dash and longer ones are used to show that something is missing, for example if you don't want to give someone's full name.	*Kim W—— was arrested today.*
definite article	The. See *article*.	*The* dream that Martin Luther King had was about true equality and freedom.
dependent clause	Another word for subordinate clause. You know the clause is dependent because of the presence of a conjunction or relative pronoun. See Chapters 7 and 8 and Appendix 2.	I will be coming out *unless it is raining*.
dialect	Use of language and grammar that belongs to a particular region of the country or group of people. (This is not the same as accent – it is more to do with the words used.) See Chapter 2.	In some dialects, the singular and plural forms are reversed from the Standard English version. Thus we might hear: '*We was* robbed; *it were* a travesty.'
ellipsis . . .	A punctuation mark showing missing words or a fading away.	Such an expression 'will forever *be* . . . *one* of Santa's little helpers' (Truss 2003).

finite verb	A complete verb that has a subject and a tense and also indicates person (1st, 2nd or 3rd). See especially Chapters 4 and 7.	Barbara *will be going* to the party when she *has found* a suitable costume.
fragment	An incomplete sentence, containing no finite verb, or having an unlinked joining word. See especially Chapter 7. A grammar checker will sometimes pick this up (Chapter 11).	*Being a fan of Gothic outfits.* *Though she hasn't found a good costume yet.* Neither of these would be sentences, even if they made sense in the context of the previous sentence.
full stop .	A punctuation mark used to show the end of a sentence (see Chapter 9) or an abbreviation (see Chapter 10). It is also known as a period.	This sentence should end in a full *stop.* We use good grammar, *e.g.* appropriate participles.
genitive case	The version of a noun or pronoun that shows it is possessive. This is common in some languages, but in English it has resulted in the apostrophe (and caused some confusion in the process). 'Girles' would originally have been the genitive of 'girls' – thus 'girles books'. Now, however, an apostrophe is inserted to show the missing letter (e). (See *Possessive* and Appendix 1.)	The genitive case can be seen in the following expressions: It's *Barbara's* chocolate. It's *her* chocolate. The chocolate is *hers*. The problem is *yours*. The second example shows a *possessive adjective*.
gerund	A noun made from a verb, usually a present participle.	The *changing* of the guard is a popular spectacle for tourists.
greengrocer's apostrophe	An expression used to describe the prevalence of inappropriate apostrophes used with simple plurals. See Chapter 10.	Kim painted out the apostrophes in the words: *pea's, potatoe's, and pomegranate's*.
hedging	Softening words used to reduce the level of certainty being expressed. While too much hedging can result in vagueness, it can be useful to introduce an element of doubt sometimes. Modal auxiliaries are particularly helpful for this (see Chapter 4).	Abel *may have taken* an interest in Sari.
hypercorrection	Wrong correction based on following a 'rule' that shouldn't apply. A typical example is when people want to avoid saying 'me' because they were told as children not to say 'Him and me want to go out.' A useful rule is that if you would say 'me' naturally if it were just you, then you should also do so when it is you and someone else, e.g. 'If it is up to Barbara and me, then we'll go for the chocolate.'	Some people say that '*between you and I*' is hypercorrection; others ask why 'between' should take the accusative case just because it does in Latin. 'Between you and me' is still regarded as the correct version, however.

Word	Definition and notes	Examples
hyphen -	Punctuation mark joining words or parts of words, especially to avoid confusion. See Chapter 10.	Kim wrote a *post-Horror* letter to Eddie.
idiom	The way things are said by a particular group of people. See Chapter 2.	I shall *table* an item at the meeting. (Literally, put on the table.) This is an idiom to say I shall want to talk about an issue but will not send out a paper in advance of the meeting. The verb 'to table' is not used in any other way. We do not table our cups and saucers.
indefinite article	A or an. See *article*.	'I have *a* dream' (Martin Luther King).
indefinite pronoun	Pronouns that don't stand for specific identifiable people: e.g. *any, anyone, some, something, none, each, either*, many (there is quite a long list).	You can't come on Wednesday or Thursday; *neither* is suitable. (Note that 'neither' is singular.)
infinitive	The 'to' form of the verb.	Barbara is happy *to write* in a formal style.
inflection	Variation in word ending which says something about number, person, tense, etc.	The inflection in a word such as '*writes*' shows that it is the *third person singular*.
interjection	A part of speech that covers exclamations. You are unlikely to use these in academic writing generally – though they would be of specialist interest, e.g. to anthropologists or linguists.	It has been noted that students from certain universities say '*hurrah!*' while others say '*hurray!*'.
intransitive verb	A verb that doesn't take an object. See Chapter 7. Many verbs have both transitive and intransitive forms, e.g. play, run, write, smell.	Barbara *hesitates*. Abel *complains*. Kim *disappears*.
	The possibility of a verb being either transitive or intransitive is behind the old joke: My dog's got no nose. How does he smell (transitive)? Awful! (Regarding 'smell' as intransitive.)	
inverted comma ' ' or " "	A punctuation mark always found in pairs that encloses direct speech, a quotation or words that require some other form of attention. Also known as quote or quotation mark. See Chapter 9.	Kim has a complaint about Barbara and Abel. '*They're* not behaving romantically, so how can I write my story *"Love and prepositions"?*' she asks.

metaphor	A figure of speech in which one thing is said to be another – the substitution drawing attention to particular aspects of the situation. The example uses a metaphor from law: there is no actual jury involved.	*The jury is out* over whether grammar books should describe usage or prescribe it.
misrelated participle	See *dangling participle.*	
modal auxiliaries	Verbs used to express mood – for example, showing doubt, necessity, duty. See Chapter 4.	Kim *ought to* concentrate on her dissertation instead of writing stories.
non-count noun	See *count noun.*	
non-restrictive clause	A relative clause that describes rather than defines part of the main clause. See Chapters 8 and 9. It usually follows a comma or is enclosed in a pair of commas.	Abel now owns a thesaurus, *which has contributed to his problems.*
noun	A word that names a person, thing, place, idea, emotion. Nouns can be abstract, i.e. they do not refer to an actual physical thing.	*Scientists* tend to prefer abstract *nouns* to *verbs*; thus they will talk about a *substitution* rather than say 'we substituted'.
noun clause	A subordinate clause that has the function of a noun. See Appendix 1.	Barbara described *what she was going to do.*
object	The person or thing that receives the action of a verb. There are also indirect objects, where someone or something is affected by the action, e.g. Barbara in example 2. See Chapter 7.	Kim plays *the saxophone*. Abel gives Barbara *a chocolate.*
parenthesis	The act of enclosing, using any of the pairs of enclosing marks shown in Figure 9.1. In the plural, it also refers to the round brackets *(parentheses)* used to enclose an aside.	The following list uses parentheses to indicate responsibility: buying Kim's bag and chocolate *(Barbara)*; tidying Kim's flat *(Derek)*; making a final check of Kim's dissertation *(Abel).*
participle	A part of a verb. For more details see 'past participle' and 'present participle'. See also Chapter 3.	The participles of the verb 'to write' are '*writing*' and '*written*'.
passive voice	The form of a verb where the subject has something done to it. Compare 'active' and see Chapter 5.	Abel *was questioned* about his timekeeping.
past participle	A part of the verb used to make up tenses and also the passive voice. In regular verbs, it ends in -d or -ed, but there are many irregular verbs. See Chapter 3 and 4.	We have *worked* well and have *written* a lot. We were *praised* for this yesterday and are *expected* to do more today.

Word	Definition and notes	Examples
perfect tense	The tense of a verb that expresses completion in the past. See Chapter 4.	Kim *has written* her speech.
period .	Another word for 'full stop'.	A sentence ends with a *period*.
person	The form of the verb and its associated subject that indicates who or what is involved. First: *I am, we are* Second: *you are* Third: *he/ she/ it/one is, they/ everybody are*	Essays should be written in the third person; that is, there should be no use of the words *I, we* or *you*.
phrase	A group of words that goes together but does not contain a verb.	The phrase '*terms of reference*' is a useful one to think about in report writing.
plagiarism	Passing off someone's work as one's own. It is mentioned in Chapter 2 because of the dangers of using a thesaurus to substitute some words for others; this would still be considered plagiarism.	If I said that a subordinate clause is one of *Santa's little assistants*, I would be plagiarizing Martin Jarvis and Lynne Truss. The expression 'Santa's little helper' is an example of idiom, and that would give me away.
pluperfect	The tense used to show action before another action already in the past.	Barbara *had met* Mark at a party and was annoyed when he didn't keep in touch.
possessive	Showing that one thing belongs to or relates to another. The genitive case is also known as the possessive case.	Possessives can be seen in adjectives (*my*), pronouns (*mine*) and nouns (the *students'* grammar).
possessive adjective	When a possessive pronoun is before a noun, then it is often called a possessive adjective.	It is *my* understanding that *his* decision is to go.
possessive pronoun	Pronouns that indicate possession may be used as adjectives (as above) or may stand alone. This is possibly where some confusion comes in, especially if the word ends up being similar to another. See *pronoun* and Appendix 1.	It is *her* decision. The decision is *hers*. She's *nobody's* fool.
predicate	What is said about the subject of a sentence, including a verb.	The students *like to study grammar occasionally* but they *prefer to watch football and go to parties*.

preposition	A word showing relationship between nouns (or their equivalent) – e.g. position, movement etc., circumstances. They often occur in phrases and may include more than one word – e.g. *in front of*.	International students are often confused with idiom associated with prepositions: *by* mistake *in* error *on* purpose interest *in* objection *to* enthusiasm *for*
present participle	A part of the verb used to make up continuous forms of tenses. It ends in -ing. It is often the cause of sentence fragments and students sometimes have problems spelling the word. See Chapter 3, especially Figure 3.1, and Chapter 7.	Kim has been *writing* a romantic story about Barbara and Abel.
pronoun	A word that stands instead of a noun. There are several different kinds: personal, indefinite, demonstrative, interrogative, and relative. They may be subjects, objects or possessive. See Appendix 1.	*I* have been writing a story about students *whose* grammar needs some work. *I* have tried to make *them* realistic. *This* is because grammar should be part of life, not separated from *it*.
question mark ?	The punctuation mark that should be used at the end of a question. An indirect question does not need one: 'Barbara asked if she could bring her sister to the party.'	'How many students are going to the party*?*' Barbara asked.
quotation mark ' ' or " "	Another name for inverted commas.	'*Can I bring my sister to the party?*' Barbara asked.
relative pronoun	A pronoun that indicates a relationship with a noun or pronoun in another part of the sentence. It is used to introduce a subordinate (adjectival) clause. See especially Chapter 8, Appendix 1 and Appendix 2.	This is the brother *who* invited his friend to the party. Eddie, *who* is Kim's brother, is studying law in Edinburgh. This is the house *that* Jack built.
restrictive clause	A clause introduced by a relative pronoun that defines or restricts the noun (or equivalent) in the main clause.	This is the brother *who invited his friend to the party*. This is the house *that Jack built*.
run-on sentence	A sentence that should be separated from the previous one by a conjunction or appropriate punctuation (not a comma). Alternatively, the sentence could be turned into a phrase.	*Barbara has not done enough studying for her exam, this is because she spends too much time on learning grammar.* The above is a run-on sentence that would be better if it were shorter. 'This' (subject) and 'is' (verb) make the clause a main one. If these words are removed, then there is no run-on sentence.

Word	Definition and notes	Examples
scare quotes ' ' or " "	Inverted commas (quotation marks) used to indicate some doubt about a term or to suggest that this is not conventional usage. Use sparingly, if at all.	This is not what '*educated*' speakers do.
semicolon ;	A punctuation mark that separates. It is particularly used in complex lists to mark a longer pause than a comma. It is also sometimes used in place of a conjunction to avoid run-on sentences. See especially Chapters 7 and 9.	Kim has invited Mark to her party; *this* is because he rescued her.
shall or will	Traditionally, it was considered correct to use 'shall' for the first person and 'will' for the second and third. The reverse was then for emphasis. This is made even more complicated by some dialect uses (e.g. Scots and Irish) that do it the other way round. (I shouldn't worry too much about this one!)	The old joke goes that a Scotsman or Irishman (depending on your prejudice) was seen in a loch or lough and heard to say: I *will* drown and no one *shall* save me. and the pedantic people on the shore thought that he wanted to drown and left him to it.
split infinitive	It is considered by some people to be inappropriate to split the 'to' form of a verb, as in the Star Trek example '*To boldly go*'. Most grammar books suggest that this is pedantry, though it often sounds better if it is avoided.	The position of an adverb can have a major impact on meaning. It may even be appropriate to split an infinitive. I only decided to go yesterday. I decided only to go yesterday. I decided *to only go* yesterday. I decided to go only yesterday.
Standard English	The dialect of English that is regarded as educated. It is taught in schools and used in formal situations. Unlike other dialects, it is not exclusively associated with a region of the country.	No-one says this outwith Scotland. 'Outwith' is a Scottish word. The Standard English version would be: No one says this *outside* Scotland. (This may change; 'outwith' could possibly eventually be absorbed into Standard English.)
subject	The person, thing or idea that a sentence or clause is about. The agent for the verb. See Chapter 6. The subject of the sentence might be a phrase or even a clause (see Appendix 2).	In olden days, *teachers* were treated with great respect. *What Abel is doing* makes Barbara very worried.
subjunctive	The subjunctive form of a verb is used to express uncertainty or possibility. It is becoming rare, except for very specific phrases.	'Far *be* it from me to question your grammar,' Barbara said to Eddie, 'but if I *were* you, I'd check my relative clauses.'

subordinate clause	A clause that cannot function as a sentence by itself. See Chapters 7 and 8. There are different types of subordinate clauses, relating to their function in a sentence: as a noun, an adjective or an adverb. See Appendix 2.	It is useful to know about subordinate clauses *because you might have too many of them.* The above is an adverbial clause – saying something about the verb in the main clause.
subordinating conjunction	A conjunction that introduces a subordinate clause.	*Although* Kim has been working hard, she still hasn't finished her dissertation.
synonym	A word that means the same as another. This is not as common as people might think; there are many shades of meaning, so it often refers to very nearly the same meaning rather than exactly the same.	In some situations, 'dishevelled' would be a synonym for 'abandoned', but only when talking about hair or clothing.
syntax	Grammatical structure in sentences. Most of this book is about syntax.	The lecturer thought that the following sentences showed <u>poor use of syntax</u>: *The essay explores the relationship of power to status, it goes without saying that this is important. Being what is likely to give people power.*
tense	The form of a verb that indicates the time of the action.	Some books suggest that there are only two tenses: present (he *writes*) and past (he *wrote*). All other situations use auxiliary verbs.
thesaurus	A book that is systematically arranged so that it is easy to find synonyms or closely related words – and their opposite (antonyms). It is important to use the punctuation of the lists as guidance to find closely related words; if you don't understand a word, it may not be an idiomatic replacement.	Here is what Roget's Thesaurus (1962) says about the word *dictionary*: '*rhyming d., polyglot d.; lexicon, wordbook, wordstock, word-list, glossary, vocabulary; thesaurus, gradus; compilation, concordance.*'
topic sentence	The example opposite shows this paragraph's topic sentence in italics.	*The topic sentence is the sentence in a paragraph that tells you what it is about.* The other sentences extend it or exemplify it. It frequently comes first in the paragraph but may come at the end.

Word	Definition and notes	Examples
transitive verb	A verb that takes an object. Some verbs are both transitive and intransitive; others, such as 'like' or 'bring' are always transitive. See Chapter 7 and *intransitive verb* earlier. Some verbs that are in phrases are always transitive, e.g. 'wait for'. Unlike intransitive verbs, transitive ones can be made passive, though this gets awkward with phrases.	Barbara *likes* Abel. Barbara *looks forward to* the party.
verb	The word denoting action in a sentence. There may be more than one verb, but there must be at least one and it should be finite (complete). See especially Chapters 4, 6 and 7, and Appendix 1.	Abel *studies* science. Barbara *is* a Gemini. Kim *benefits from* her friends.
voice	A way of categorizing verbs to show their relationship with the subject: active or passive.	By using the *passive voice*, I can either hide the agent or draw attention to it. The soldier *was executed*. The soldier *was executed* by his own general.
who or whom	Who is used as the subject of the verb; whom is used as the object.	Barbara called the shopowner *who* had threatened Kim. Barbara called the shopowner *whom* Kim had offended.

Appendix 1: More details on parts of speech

Grammar books often use examples that we never see in real life. This Appendix uses examples from books to illustrate some additional points. As my comments show, it is not always clear how to classify things, but what matters more is how well the logic of the sentence works for the reader.

The basic logic relates to verbs and their subjects – which may be nouns, pronouns or their equivalent. Adverbs and adjectives say something else about verbs and nouns.

Verbs

A strong message in this book is that a sentence should contain a verb. That is the main thing to remember: if your sentence sounds odd, is that because a verb or part of a verb is missing?

What counts as a verb? The expression 'a verb is a doing word' may not be very helpful, as sometimes that doing is just existing or even just helping to complete other verbs. It is also possible to see action in bits of verbs that are not complete in themselves.

These and other issues are illustrated in the following passage, where the finite (complete) verbs are italicized.

He *was* systematic, but to say he *thought* and *acted* like a machine *would be to misunderstand* the nature of his thought. It *was not* like pistons and wheels and gears all moving at once, massive and co-ordinated. The image of a laser beam *comes* to mind instead; a single pencil of light of such terrific energy in such extreme concentration it *can be shot at* the moon and its reflection *[can be] seen* back on earth. Phaedrus *did not try to use* his brilliance for general illumination. He *sought* one specific distant target and *aimed for* it and *hit* it. And that *was* all. General illumination of that target he *hit* now *seems to be left for* me.

(Pirsig 1974: 80)

This passage illustrates a number of points I want to add about verbs.

Phrasal verb: A verb might have an adverb or preposition that is a part of its meaning: *was not; can be shot at; aimed for; seems to be left for.* This is known as a phrasal verb. Some commentators are frowning on the tendency to create unnecessary phrasal verbs, for example *meet with* rather than meet.

Transitive and intransitive: All but the first of those phrasal verbs in the previous paragraph are transitive – that is, they need an object. There are some intransitive phrasal verbs; for example, 'aim high', 'go away'. The main reason for pointing this out is to stress that some verbs do need to have objects and some don't. Some verbs can be transitive or intransitive depending on the context, for example: *My car broke down* (intransitive). *Kim broke down the argument for Abel* (transitive).

Finite and infinitive: In the first sentence in the example, the expression 'to say' is not a finite verb; it is an infinitive. The infinitive, with or without the word 'to', is the form of the verb that has no *inflection* – that is, it does not by itself show time or person. As was shown in Chapter 4, the infinitive can be used to make up finite verbs, as can the past and present participles. In the example here, the infinitive 'to say' is used as a subject for the verb 'would be to misunderstand' (which itself contains an infinitive).

Nouns

Nouns name things, ideas and people. I'm using the following passage to highlight three types of noun – concrete, abstract, proper. I have italicized all the nouns.

> *Rahel* was first blacklisted in *Nazareth Covent* at the age of eleven, when she was caught outside her *Housemistress's* garden *gate* decorating a *knob* of fresh *cowdung* with small *flowers.* At *Assembly* the next *morning* she was made to look up *depravity* in the *Oxford Dictionary* and read aloud its *meaning.* 'The quality or condition of being depraved or corrupt,' *Rahel* read, with a row of stern-mouthed *nuns* seated behind her and a *sea* of sniggering schoolgirl *faces* in front.
>
> (Roy 1997: 16)

Concrete nouns:	gate, knob, cowdung, flowers, nuns, sea, faces.
Abstract nouns:	morning (?) depravity, quality, condition
Proper nouns:	Rahel, Nazareth Convent, Housemistress's,
	Assembly (?). Oxford Dictionary

As always, it is the exceptions or the tricky examples that make us think about the way we classify things. I wondered about 'morning' – it does not seem very concrete. But it doesn't quite fit the usual idea of abstract nouns either.

Eventually, I decided that it is a construct, rather than a physical thing. However, although 'sea' is a metaphor, it is still a concrete one.

I have also put a question mark at Assembly as it would not usually be regarded as a 'proper' noun – a formal name. However, it has been used this way here as has Housemistress, and this can be seen by the capital letter.

I decided not to include 'front' as a noun as it is really a preposition 'in front'. Again, not everyone would necessarily agree with this approach. The word 'schoolgirl', while normally a noun, is here being used as an adjective.

Abstract nouns refer to things that we cannot perceive through our senses, but are used to express ideas. Too many of them can be very confusing: in fact, the idea of 'depravity' probably doesn't mean very much to a little girl, in spite of the dictionary definition. Much academic writing contains many abstract nouns, some say unnecessarily. If you find you have a lot of words ending in -ness or -tion, then you perhaps have too many of them.

The other point to make about nouns is that some can be counted and others cannot. In the earlier passage, the words 'cowdung' and 'depravity' cannot be counted (you would not make them plural, for example). Nouns that can't be counted are never used with 'a' or 'an' (*indefinite articles*). You would not say 'a cowdung' or 'a depravity'. However, you can say 'some cowdung' and 'some depravity'. This point often causes problems for non-native English speakers.

Count nouns can cause problems for native English speakers too, however. The following are the ones that most purists get excited about.

I've had a great *amount* of trouble (*non-count*).
I've had a great *number* of difficulties (count).

I have *less* coal for my fire than you (non-count).
I have *fewer* sticks for my fire than you (count).

This is why the sign in the supermarket should say: 'Ten items or fewer'. If you can count them, then the word is 'fewer'.

Pronouns

Pronouns stand instead of nouns. There are various different types of pronoun: personal, possessive, reflexive, demonstrative, relative, interrogative, and indefinite. The passage below contains examples of the first four of these.

Ruth now pushed *her* cart toward the fish counter. *She* longed for prawns in the shell, always *her* first choice. Art wouldn't eat *them*, however. *He* claimed that the predominant taste of any crustacean or mollusk was *that* of *its* alimentary tract. *She* settled on Chilean sea bass. 'That one,' *she* told the man at the counter. Then *she* reconsidered: 'Actually, give *me* the bigger one.' *She* might as well ask *her* mother to dinner, since *they* were already going to the doctor's together. Luling was always complaining *she* didn't like to cook for just *herself*.

(Tan 2001: 34)

In the example, we can see the following:

Personal pronouns: *she, he, they, me, them.* The words 'me' and 'them' are the accusative case of I and they respectively.
Possessive pronouns: *her, its.* As these have come before a noun, they are more likely to be called possessive adjectives (or determiners). But strictly they are still possessive pronouns. Note the change if the first example had come after the noun – e.g. the choice was hers.
Reflexive pronoun: *herself.* These are used to refer back to the subject, or they may just be used for emphasis. In the example, it refers back to the subject of the subordinate clause.

Figure A1 is a chart with all the personal, possessive and reflexive pronouns. This chart shows the correct versions of some expressions that are frequently confused with others. Notice in particular that the only word that contains an apostrophe is 'one's' – which is most likely to be used as a possessive adjective, e.g. *One has the greatest respect for one's teachers.*
The passage also showed another type of pronoun.

Demonstrative pronoun: *that* (in 'that of its alimentary tract') – the pronoun

	First person	Second person	Third person
Personal – as subject	I, we	you, you	he, she, it, one, they
Personal – as object	me, us	you, you	him, her, it, one, them
Possessive pronoun	mine, ours	yours, yours	his, hers, its (rare), one's (rare), their
Possessive adjective (before a noun)	my, our	your, your	his, her, its, one's, their
Reflexive pronoun	myself, ourselves	yourself, yourself	himself, herself, itself, oneself, themselves

FIGURE A.1 Pronouns and person.

refers back to the noun 'taste'. It is always important to be clear what *this, that, these* or *those* refer back to when the words are being used as pronouns. 'That' can be a demonstrative pronoun, a relative pronoun or a demonstrative adjective. In the passage, 'that' in 'that one' is being used as an adjective and 'one' is being used as a noun.

There are some other types of pronoun that are not illustrated in that passage.

Relative pronouns: These are considered in detail in Chapter 8. The relative pronouns are: *who, whom, whose, which, what, that* (also *whoever, whichever* etc.).

Interrogative pronouns: These are the pronouns that are used to start a question, and because of this they are not usually referring back to a noun. The interrogative pronouns are: *Who, Whom, Whose, What, Which* and I have used capitals to show that they are likely to come at the start of a sentence.

Indefinite pronouns: These are words such as *someone, everyone, all, many, no one, none, each, either* . . . it's a very long list. The main point made with indefinite pronouns is to watch for the appropriate verb ending. Some are treated as third person singular: *neither of us has studied grammar; each is keen to learn.* Others, such as 'some' or 'many' are third person plural.

Adjectives

Some of the classifications above apply to adjectives as well as pronouns. I have already made the case for possessive adjectives; there are also demonstrative, relative and interrogative ones. Here are some examples. In each case, you should put a noun after them – for example, books.

> **Possessive adjectives:** *my, your, his, her, its, our, your, their*
> **Demonstrative adjectives:** *this, that, these, those*
> **Relative adjectives:** *whose* (e.g. Kim is the person whose book I borrowed); *which* (e.g. for which purpose, in which case)
> **Interrogative adjectives:** *Which* books are they? *Whose* books are they? *What* books do you want?

This shows that adjectives go beyond the obvious descriptive words, such as *pretty, blue,* and *good.* Again, the points here are mainly made to help you to avoid confusion and recognize that expressions such as its book and whose book are perfectly correct. It is probably unnecessary to remember the classifications themselves.

Numbers are also adjectives when they are used with nouns – for example, twenty books, one prize. It is worth mentioning number, because of the point made earlier about count nouns. Some adjectives are not appropriate for count nouns and others for non-count nouns. Some, however, are OK for both as the set below shows.

Count noun	Non-count noun	Count	Non-count
few items	little hope	many items	much hope
fewer items	less hope	more items	more hope
fewest items	least hope	most items	most hope

The example above also shows the comparison of few, little, many and much. The comparison of adjectives often works in the same way as 'few' – for example, dull, duller, dullest. But there are some other irregular comparisons:

good	bad
better	worse
best	worst

For long adjectives, it more usual to write 'more' or 'most': curious, more curious, most curious.

Note that you don't have a comparative or superlative for some adjectives, or you shouldn't. Many people make errors with 'unique'. Either something is unique or it isn't; there aren't degrees of it.

Adverbs

> In fact, it would be tempting to say that grammarians call a word an 'adverb' if they cannot confidently describe it as anything else.
>
> (Kahn 1985: 24)

The concern above arises because adverbs don't just modify verbs. They can also modify other adverbs, adjectives, phrases, clauses or sentences. While they often end in -ly, there are many examples that do not. (And some words that end in -ly are adjectives, e.g. 'friendly'.) In addition, many words are adverbs as well as other things, such as prepositions, adjectives or conjunctions.

Despite their complexity, it is useful to think about adverbs because they do some important work in the logic of sentences, especially when they turn into phrases or clauses (see Appendix 2). In the passage below, however, I have just highlighted the single-word adverbs.

> It was the White Rabbit, trotting *slowly* back again, and looking *anxiously* about it as it went, as if it had lost something; and she heard it muttering

to itself 'The Duchess! The Duchess! Oh my dear paws! Oh my fur and whiskers! She'll get me executed, as sure as ferrets are ferrets! *Where* can I have dropped them, I wonder?' Alice guessed in a moment that it was looking for the fan and the pair of white kid gloves, and she *very good-naturedly* began hunting about for them, but they were *nowhere* to be seen – everything seemed to have changed since her swim in the pool, and the great hall, with the glass table and the little door, had vanished *completely*.

(Carroll, L. 1865/1946: 52)

The passage shows the following examples:

Adverbs of manner: slowly, anxiously, good-naturedly
Adverbs of degree: very, completely
Adverb of place: nowhere
Interrogative adverb: Where . . .?

Palmer (2003) provides a classification of seven types of adverb: manner; place; time; degree, quantity or extent; number; relative; interrogative. Let's look at how each of these can be used to say something about the way our students do things.

Manner:	Barbara uses correct participles *automatically*.
Place:	Kim went to the football and met Abel *there*.
Time:	*Yesterday*, Abel had an upset stomach.
Degree:	Barbara has *nearly* finished reading Kim's dissertation.
Number:	Barbara asked Abel *twice* to get a birthday card.
Relative:	Abel asked *where* the film would be shown.
Interrogative:	*Why* did Barbara not ask Abel out?

Sometimes adverbs can be moved around and this can change the meaning. Consider the sentence:

Barbara has corrected Kim's dissertation.

If we add the adverb 'probably' to this sentence, its position will change the meaning:

Probably Barbara has corrected Kim's dissertation. Abel has not.
Barbara probably has corrected Kim's dissertation. She is likely to have finished it.
Barbara has probably corrected Kim's dissertation. It wouldn't have been correct otherwise.

The meaning depends partly on context, but moving an adverb around can certainly change the emphasis. It may even change it from an adverb of time to one of manner or extent. (See also the example under 'Split infinitive' in the Glossary.)

Some adverbs can be compared, like adjectives (though you don't of course get 'more yesterday' and 'most yesterday'!) Look at the following comparisons:

nearly	more nearly	most nearly
probably	more probably	most probably
fast	faster	fastest
well	better	best

People are often unsure of whether they are using adverbs or adjectives (and some words are genuinely ambiguous). *Abel left early in the afternoon* uses early as an adverb; *Abel left in the early afternoon* uses it as an adjective.

'Well' is an adjective, usually talking about health. *Abel is feeling well now*.

It is also an adverb. *Abel has done well in his essay*. The problem with 'well' is that its comparative and superlative are the same as those for 'good'. But good is an adjective and not an adverb. Though you can say, *Abel is feeling good now*, it would be wrong to replace 'well' in the other sentence with good: *Abel has done ~~good~~ well in his essay*. (This is, however, a very common error.)

Appendix 2: More details on clauses

A clause always contains a verb and usually a subject (though that may not be actually expressed). A group of words that goes together but does not contain a verb is known as a phrase. It is useful to think of clauses and phrases together because it might be appropriate to turn a clause into a phrase or *vice versa*.

There are three different types of subordinate clause, according to the work that they do in a sentence:

- **adverbial clauses**, that usually comment on the verb in the main clause; these are particularly discussed in Chapter 7; although the expression was not used there;
- **adjectival clauses**, usually known as **relative clauses**; these are particularly discussed in Chapter 8;
- **noun clauses**, replacing a noun in a sentence, e.g. a subject or object, which have not been discussed already.

This appendix brings the three types together so that you can compare them. I have used similar examples to help highlight the differences between them. You might want to get rid of some of your subordinate clauses; there are suggestions here for that too.

Adverbial clauses

These are clauses that take the function of an adverb. Like single-word adverbs, they might talk about manner, place, time, degree and number. They might also make observations on causes, effects, purposes and limitations.

In other words, they answer the questions: how, where, when, how much, how often, why.

They always begin with a conjunction. Here are some examples of adverbial clauses, with the conjunction underlined.

Barbara finished her essay <u>before</u> she went to the pub with Abel.
Kim wants to enter the competition <u>because</u> she needs a laptop.

Abel will go to the party <u>when</u> he stops feeling queasy.
The students put the apostrophes <u>where</u> they were needed.

Adjectival (relative) clauses

These are clauses that do the work of an adjective. They answer the questions who, which and what? They always begin with a relative pronoun.

- Barbara finished the essay <u>that</u> was due in the next day.
- Kim wants to enter the competition, <u>which</u> she hopes will win her a laptop.
- Abel, <u>who</u> is feeling queasy, will go to the party later.
- The students put the apostrophes in the words <u>whose</u> sense needed them.

Chapters 8 and 9 stressed the differences between relative clauses that define (restrictive) clauses and those that describe (non-restrictive). In the above sentences, the first and last contain restrictive clauses. This distinction is a useful one to guide your writing, but not all writers observe it.

Noun clauses

A clause can replace a noun and be used as the subject, object or complement of the sentence. Noun clauses often start with that or what but there are a number of other possibilities: *if, whether, how, what, when, where, which, who, whom, whose, why, however, whatever, whenever, wherever, whichever, whoever, whomever*. This list shows that they can answer a number of questions and they do use some of the same linking words as the other two types. What is important is the role they play in the sentence.

In the following sentences, I have underlined the noun clause and described its position in the sentence.

Barbara finished <u>what she was doing</u>. (object)
<u>Whoever enters the competition</u> might win a laptop. (subject)
The thought of the party later was <u>what was making Abel feel queasy</u>. (complement)
The students thought <u>that some apostrophes were missing</u>. (object)

The three different types of clause show different ways of writing about the same topics. There are other ways too; there are adverbial, adjectival and noun phrases. If you have many clauses, you might want to think about this.

Figure A.2 shows some replacements for all the examples in this section – in some cases, you can see that it is hard to capture everything with a phrase.

The main point here is that it is possible to use a variety of structures to comment on a situation. If your sentences are becoming long and convoluted, you should consider alternatives such as turning clauses into phrases. If they are becoming short and stilted, you may want to add an explanatory clause.

Using a clause...	Using a phrase...
Barbara finished her essay before she went to the pub with Abel.	Barbara finished her essay before going to the pub with Abel.
Barbara finished the essay that was due in the next day.	Barbara finished the essay for the following day.
Barbara finished what she was doing.	Barbara finished her task.
Kim wants to enter the competition because she needs a laptop.	Kim, needing a laptop, wants to enter the competition.
Kim wants to enter the competition, which she hopes will win her a laptop.	Kim wants to enter the competition, hoping to win a laptop.
Whoever enters the competition might win a laptop.	Competition entrants might win a laptop.
Abel will go to the party when he stops feeling queasy.	Abel will go to the party when appropriate.
Abel, who is feeling queasy, will go to the party later.	Because of his queasy feeling, Abel will go to the party later.
The thought of the party later was what was making Abel feel queasy.	The thought of the party later was the cause of Abel's queasiness.
The students put the apostrophes where they were needed.	The students put the apostrophes where necessary.
The students put the apostrophes in the words whose sense needed them.	The students put the apostrophes in the appropriate words.
The students thought that some apostrophes were missing.	The students thought about missing apostrophes.

FIGURE A.2 Clauses and phrases.

Appendix 3: Warning signs

If you are constantly thinking about grammar as you write, there is a danger that you won't get anything written. While you're writing, the questions, **'What exactly am I trying to say?'** and, **'What's going on?'** are useful ones. If you're getting stuck and it doesn't sound right, perhaps you should ask yourself, **'Is there a subject, verb, object?'** and, **'Which words are my signposts?'** It may even be useful to ask, **'Am I completing, introducing, separating, enclosing or omitting?'** However, for many people, some of these questions are best left for the stage of checking over for sense. (See Figure 1.1.)

As you get used to some of the ideas talked about in this book, you may begin to find yourself responding to warning signs. In Figure A.3, I have listed things that trigger a warning for me, both when I am writing and when I am proofreading. These are things that I know can often go wrong.

I've included this short list to encourage you to make your own. If you know you make the same mistakes over and over again, you need to try to find a way to avoid it or ensure that you pick it up in proofreading. There are further examples of frequent errors in Burt (2004) (see Bibliography).

Often, of course, the real problem is that the student has not had time to proofread the essay properly. Although it looks like one, it's not a grammar problem at all!

What I might write	What might be wrong	Comment
there	Perhaps it should be 'their' or 'they're'	Best to make it 'they are', rather than 'they're'
,	It might not be strong enough or it might not be necessary.	I make this kind of decision at proofreading stage
definitely	I might spell it with an a instead of the second i	It has 'finite' in the middle
separate	I might spell it with an e instead of the first a	It has 'pair' without the i in the middle
desperate	I might spell it with an a instead of the second e	I remember the Latin for 'I hope' is 'spero' – this helps me to spell it.
it's	It should be 'its'	Never write 'it's' – replace it with 'it is'
where	It should be 'were'	Actually, I don't do this. Because I have a Scottish accent, I 'hear' a difference between these two words. But so many students, including Scottish ones, do this that I thought I'd put it in the list.
a very long sentence	There are many unnecessary words.	I do this one a lot. I then go back over it to see if I can shorten it.

FIGURE A.3 Warning signs.

Bibliography

I consulted many books and several internet sites to help me to write this book. Some of the following are referenced within the book, others are not. This is a list of my own recommendations, but there are many other excellent examples too.

Amis, K. (1997) *The King's English*. London: HarperCollins.
> Kingsley Amis was himself an excellent writer who had strong, often controversial, views. This book doesn't pull any punches, but does encourage us to steer an appropriate course between the sloppy and overly punctilious.

Burchfield, R. (ed.) *The New Fowler's Modern English Usage*, third edn. Oxford: Clarendon Press.
> There are several editions of this classic reference book. There are debates about whether this edition preserves the ethos of Fowler's original work. It both records the changing uses of English and makes recommendations for 'correct' usage.

Burt, A. (2004) *Quick Solutions to Common Errors in English*. Oxford: How to Books Ltd.
> There are many mistakes in spelling, punctuation and grammar that students make repeatedly. Burt lists them alphabetically and offers useful tips on getting them right.

Chambers Dictionary (2003) Edinburgh: Chambers.
> Chambers is my favourite dictionary, but this is a personal choice and there are many other good ones.

Collinson, D., Kirkup, G., Kyd, R. and Slocombe, L. (1992) *Plain English*, second edn. Buckingham: Open University Press.
> There are some useful quizzes and advice on typical problems in spelling, punctuation and grammar.

Crystal, D. (1987) *The Cambridge Encyclopaedia of Language*. Cambridge: Cambridge University Press.
> This is the edition referenced in Chapter 7; a later one is available. It is a fascinating book, so it can be distracting.

Gowers, E. (1973) (Revised by Sir Bruce Fraser) *The Complete Plain Words*. London: HMSO.
> This is a classic book for civil servants to encourage them to write clearly. It is itself well-written and contains some lovely examples.

Kahn, J. (1985) (ed.) *The Right Word at the Right Time*. London: The Readers Digest Association Ltd.
> I bought this book in a second hand bookshop a few years ago and have found it invaluable as a reference book and also a source of diverting articles – e.g. on 'English around the world'. I was interested to see that Palmer also references it.

Kipfer, B.A. (ed.) (2006) *Roget's New Millennium™ Thesaurus*, first edn. (V 1.3.1), Lexico Publishing Group, LLC.
> This is the most recent version of Roget's Thesaurus, though an older version was referred to in the Glossary. There is an associated website at http://thesaurus. reference.com/

Palmer, R. (2003) *The Good Grammar Guide*. London: Routledge.
> This is a particularly helpful book for students and I like Palmer's down-to-earth style.

Peck, J. and Coyle, M. (1999) *The Student's Guide to Writing*. Basingstoke: Macmillan.
> The authors present a very practical guide for students, containing useful summaries of key issues in grammar, punctuation and spelling.

Truss, L. (2003) *Eats, Shoots & Leaves*. London: Profile Books.
> This is a book to read when you have become passionate about punctuation and want to preserve high standards. It's also very funny; but you do need to understand why the author is taking such a stance.

The following books provided examples for analysis.

Bloom, H. (1994) *The Western Canon*. London: Papermac.

Bryson, B. (2003) *A Short History of Nearly Everything*. London: Black Swan.

Carroll, L. (1865/1946) *Alice's Adventures in Wonderland*. Harmondsworth: Penguin Books.

Dickens, C. (1837/1963) *The Pickwick Papers*. London: Collins.

Kemp Smith, N. (translator) (1933) *Immanuel Kant's Critique of Pure Reason*, second impression. London: Macmillan and Co. Ltd.

Pirsig, R.(1974) *Zen and the Art of Motorcycle Maintenance*. Aylesbury: Corgi Books.

Roy, A. (1997) *The God of Small Things*. London: Flamingo.

Silver, B. (1998) *The Ascent of Science*. Oxford: Oxford University Press.

Tan, A. (2001) *The Bonesetter's Daughter*. London: Flamingo.

Wright, P. (1994) *Introduction to Engineering*, second edn. New York: John Wiley and Sons.

An example of one of many useful websites is the Online Writing Lab at Purdue University:

owl.english.purdue.edu/handouts/grammar/

Finally, the CD track 'Phonetic Punctuation' that Abel and Kim enjoyed so much can be heard on Victor Borge *Phonetically Speaking – And Don't Forget the Piano!* Jasmine Records 2001.

Index

Understanding University

A Guide to Another Planer

Christine Sinclair

- Does university seem like another planet?
- Does everyone else seem to speak another language?
- What can you do to make the grade?

If these are the kind of questions you are asking, then this is the book you need. After the excitement of being accepted, the reality of life at university or college can be daunting, but help is at hand. This practical book guides new students through the terminology used at university and shows you:

- What a student needs to know
- How to be accepted by students and lecturers
- How to get the best out of your institution and yourself
- How to communicate using appropriate language in higher education institutions
- How to learn the conventions of your specific subject area
- How to be confident and competent in your new world

All new students find the move to university slightly bewildering, but with this book you can be one step ahead. The author has spent time talking to students across a broad range of different universities and uses her first-hand experience as a basis for the book.

Understanding University provides a lifeline for new students in further and higher education offering everything from practical advice on studying, to explanations of frequently used terms. If you don't know the difference between a seminar and a tutorial or want to know what 'matriculation' means, then this is where to start.

Need a little assistance? Just open this book. And remember – you are not alone.

2006   176pp
ISBN-13: 978–0–335–21797–7 ISBN-10: 0–335–21797–4 Paperback
ISBN-13: 978–0–335–21798–4 ISBN-10: 0–335–21798–2- Hardback

STUDENT FRIENDLY GUIDES

WRITE GREAT ESSAYS!

Peter Levin

Reading and essay writing for undergraduate and taught postgraduate students

What every student needs for university reading and writing!

- How can students find what they need from the long lists of recommended reading?
- What kind of notes should they take?
- What is the best way to structure an essay?
- How can plagiarism be avoided?

This lively, short, and to-the-point guide helps students to study and write effectively. Practical hints and suggestions which really work are coupled with insights into academic writing, critical reading and methods of presentation.

This guide builds confidence and changes study habits so students can get the grades they really deserve for the work they put in. No student should be without it!

Contents

The strange world of the university. READ THIS FIRST! – Introduction – Part One: Getting started – 'I'm a slow reader' – Three stages in academic learning – Coping with monster reading lists – Part Two: Reading purposes and strategies – What are you reading for? – Making notes and translating 'academic-speak' – 6 Exploratory reading: How to summarize a publication – Dedicated reading: How to make the material 'yours' – Part Three: Targeted reading – The principles behind targeted reading – How to identify key terms – How to scan a book – Part Four: Writing essays – Discovering what's wanted from you – How to clarify your topic – Thinking it through: a note on methodology – An all-purpose plan – Using quotations – The writing process – Part Five: Referencing systems – Using and citing sources – Which system to choose? – Recording details of your sources – Part Six: Plagiarism and collusion – The conscientious student's predicament – How academic learning forces you to plagiarize – Avoiding accusations of plagiarism – The politics of plagiarism

136pp   0 335 21577 7 (Paperback)

STUDENT FRIENDLY GUIDES

SUCCESSFUL TEAMWORK!

Peter Levin

This short, practical guide is for students who find themselves placed in groups and assigned a project to carry out.

- Allocating work appropriately
- Dealing with people who are taking a 'free-ride'
- Resolving disagreements
- Working constructively with people who they don't like very much.

The guide helps students to appreciate the tensions between the demands of the task, the needs of the team and individual's needs, and to understand why people behave as they do in a team situation. It provides reassurance when things get stressful, and helps students learn from the experience and make a success of their project.

Contents

Part One: Basics and Context – What do we mean by 'a team'? – The benefits of working in a team – Teamwork skills – Academic teamwork and the job market – Part Two: Getting Started – Get in your groups – Get to know one another – Formulate your ground rules – Check out your assignment and plan your work – Part Three: How are we Doing? – Progress on the project – Progress from 'group' to 'team' – Personal progress – Part Four: Perspectives on Team Behaviour – Tensions: the task, the team and the individual – Team roles – Management systems and team organization – Team development: forming, storming, norming, performing . . . – The decision-making process – Negotiation – Cultural traits and differences – Individual traits: 'cats' and 'dogs' – Part Five: Teamwork Issues and Solutions – The task: getting the work done – Personal and inter-personal issues – Part Six: Benefiting from the Experience – Getting feedback – Reflection – Applying for jobs

136pp   0 335 21578 5 (Paperback)